# SHEPHERDS, HIRELINGS AND DICTATORS

# SHEPHERDS, HIRELINGS AND DICTATORS

HOW TO RECOGNIZE THE DIFFERENCE

## TAVARES D. ROBINSON

Watchman PUBLISHING

Published by Watchman Publishing
www.watchmanpublishing.com

Watchman Publishing is a Christian publisher that seeks to edify the local church by equipping individuals. We provide resources to admonish, exhort, reprove and encourage the church in the Last Days.

Shepherds, Hirelings and Dictators: *How to Recognize the Difference*

Unless otherwise indicated, all Scripture references are taken from the New King James Version®. Copyright © 1982 by Thomas Nelson, Inc.

Scripture quotations marked NLT are taken from the *Holy Bible*, New Living Translation, copyright © 1996 by Tyndale House Publishers, Inc.

Printed in the United States of America/ First Edition: 2010, Second Edition: 2020

ISBN 978-1-7325134-6-4 (trade paper), ISBN 978-1-7325134-7-1 (e-book)

Cover photography and design by Jesus Cordero

Editors: Leonard G. Goss and Carolyn Stanford Goss, GoodEditors.com, www.goodeditors.com

# ACKNOWLEDGMENTS

I would like to send my sincere thanks and gratitude to everyone, who over these last ten years, have supported me whether it was through editing, encouraging words, personal testimonies, monetary giving, and especially their heartfelt prayers. I pray that the Lord would remember your kindness and generosity towards his work.

And most importantly, I would like to thank my Lord and Savior Jesus Christ for extending his grace towards me in trusting me with his eternal truths. May the Lamb of God receive the reward of his suffering.

# CONTENTS

# FOREWORD

Deception is rampant in the church. We must confront it boldly, without fear, and *Shepherds, Hirelings and Dictators* helps us do just that. This book is an excellent and much needed source written by a godly pastor who loves the body of Christ and yet sees a massive apostasy and departure from the pure gospel of Jesus Christ. Most of this has to do with predators in the pulpit who are like savage wolves, preying upon undiscerning souls.

The apostle Paul writes these words of warning in Acts 20:27–31:

> "For I have not shunned to declare to you the whole counsel of God. Therefore take heed to yourselves and to all the flock, among which the Holy Spirit has made you overseers, to shepherd the church of God which He purchased with His own blood. For I know this, that after my departure savage wolves will come in among you, not sparing the flock. Also from among yourselves men will rise up, speaking perverse things, to draw away the disciples after themselves. Therefore watch, and remember that for three years I did not cease to warn everyone night and day with tears."

This is an earnest and urgent warning from Paul to the church. Verse 31 says he warned them for three years with tears! If this warning was valid then, it is much more valid today. To warn is to love the flock. Godly shepherds will protect the flock. This is their duty and calling from God. Wolves, on the other hand, will eat the flock. Therefore, they must be identified.

Romans 16:17 warns, "Note those who cause divisions and offenses, contrary to the doctrine which you learned, and avoid them." We must be bold in exposing the dangerous errors promoted by false teachers who sugar coat deadly poison as they teach doctrines that lead people away from the True God of the Bible.

Notice that Paul warns that these grievous wolves who do not fear God will devour the flock and that these false shepherds will teach false doctrines and seek to have people follow them instead of Christ. Paul was committed to continually warning them about this, night and day, for *three years*.

Pastor Robinson gives us serious warnings concerning hirelings—those pastors who are not genuinely called by God nor sincere about preaching truth—and dictators. Why? Well, we find the answer in 2 Peter 2:1, in which the apostle warns that false teachers shall bring in the church "destructive heresies." Yes, these destructive teachings will lead souls to hell. False ministers are teaching destructive heresies and many are being deceived by the error they hear. We must warn them.

Robinson has written a timely book that should be read by those who want the whole truth. Each chapter is filled with vital truths that will help the reader develop discernment. Let me request that if you know someone following a hireling, please consider giving them a copy of this book. God can use it to set the person free from deception.

Warnings are like setting off a fire alarm that is intended to wake people up, and Robinson knows many are spiritually asleep and need to be warned. A fire out of control spreads its deadly flames fast, causing much destruction. And biblical warnings are necessary because the destructive flames of false doctrines, taught by illegitimate ministers in the pulpit, can ruin many lives.

Friends, why did God give us his holy Word? Second Timothy 3:16 tells us, "All Scripture is given by inspiration of God, and it is profitable for doctrine, for reproof, for correction, for instruction in righteousness." We, however, hear very little reproof and correction today. In fact, false pastors avoid it altogether. Exposing sin and preaching repentance are not popular doctrines in today's seeker-friendly churches. In fact, if you preach these sound doctrines you will offend people, and that's what false pastors do not want to do. They prefer to function in the role of people pleasers who tickle itching ears.

### REPROOF

We must hear reproof that will show people what is not right in their lives. This means real men of God must preach against sin and not be afraid if it offends people. Proverbs 15:31–32 reads:

> "The ear that hears the rebukes of life will abide among the wise. He who disdains instruction despises his own soul, but he who heeds rebuke gets understanding."

### CORRECTION

If we desire to really please the Lord and walk in holiness we will want to hear a word of correction. Correction tells us how to get right with God. Proverbs 15:10 says, "Whoever abandons the right path will be severely disciplined; whoever hates correction will die" (NLT). If you reject correction and reproof you are showing you had a false conversion. This is no light matter and

*Shepherds, Hirelings, and Dictators* is a serious book that brings much needed reproof and correction.

Dear friends, we all need to understand biblical doctrines and we need men of God in the pulpit who preach wholesome teachings, not cotton candy sermons void of truth. A man of God, in his preaching, will point out things in our lives that displease the Lord. He will confront and expose error. The grace of God teaches us to live godly lives every day and the Word of God gives us all the details of what defines a godly life that honors him. Illuminating these details is one of the main goals of this book.

Multitudes are on a broad road heading to destruction because of self-anointed, self-appointed, and self-ordained ministers who lust after power, prestige, popularity, and prosperity. They do not live lives of godly purity and do not teach sound doctrine. They prove to be lovers of themselves and twist the Scripture for the purpose of selfish gain.

This book sharply rebukes such imposters and frauds. It clearly explains the true characteristics of God-called shepherds and clearly exposes the evil characteristics of hirelings and dictators. Pastor Robinson does not waste or mince his words and he makes no apologies for telling the truth that needs to be heard in these days of apostasy.

If you want to be cured you will not argue about the taste of the medicine.

### Instruction in Righteousness

I exhort the reader to study each chapter. You will be biblically informed and you will, without a doubt, know how to recognize the difference between true ministers and false ministers. Many eyes need to be opened and to be set free from the grip of hirelings and dictators, real discernment needs to be developed.

Let me conclude with this: Chapter four is short but packed with vital information that will reveal the true character of a godly, God-called pastor who fulfills the biblical requirements for leadership in the church. Study those "signs that identify true shepherds" and test those preachers you listen to, whether they are in your own church or are one of those TV preachers who many follow blindly. So-called Christian TV is full of local church programs featuring many hirelings and dictators!

I heartily endorse this book and hope that it will be widely read. Study it. Buy an extra copy and give it to your pastor. Second Corinthians 4:2 should be the motto of every minister. The God-called minister must follow Paul's example: "But we have renounced the hidden things of shame, not walking in craftiness nor handling the word of God deceitfully, but by manifestation of the truth commending ourselves to every man's conscience in the sight of God."

May the churches be filled with people of this caliber and full commitment to obey Christ. Keep pressing on in Jesus.

Serving our Risen Lord,

**–David C. Cooke, aflame4God Ministries, Richmond, Virginia**

## PREFACE, 2020 EDITION

Over the past few years I have found myself periodically revisiting this book that I wrote ten years ago. The time has gone by quickly, but from the look of things in the church, the message has been received slowly or outright rejected. Little did I know that the first book I would write would set off a firestorm in my personal life. Some friendships with other pastors—some whose pulpits I have even filled from time to time—suddenly came to an end. Some friendships that I thought would be enduring gradually faded away. People questioned my motive for the book, asking, "Why would a pastor write these things about the church?" "Why would a pastor bash other leaders?" Some even questioned why God would have me to expose the church in such a way, therefore, making it harder for sinners to get saved.

While I am on this point, it is highly important that I establish a truth: When individuals have been graced by Christ to touch on sensitive topics or confront eternally harmful teachings, they are not being critical—they are showing love! You see, too many Christians have bought into the Enemy's lie that calling untruthful teachers out will have an adverse effect on unbelievers coming to Christ.

From a biblical and theological perspective, I do not agree. Most who feel this way are measuring things from a personal point of view instead of a biblical polemics frame of mind. What do I mean by *polemics*? It is the opposite side of the coin of apologetics. Christian *apologetics* is defending the faith and the truths of Christianity among unbelievers. Christian polemics is defending the truth among those professing Christianity. Jesus was a stark defender of the truth from both external and internal attacks. He did not think denouncing the Pharisees, unauthorized and illegitimate teachers of the law, and pronouncing repetitive woes upon them in front of the crowd would hinder people from receiving the true gospel (Matt. 23:1–39).

In actuality, when questionable leaders go unchecked, we are giving them visual and auditory platforms in the church from which they can do irreparable damage leading to eternal destruction. This is exactly what our Adversary desires to accomplish; he is raising up dangerous leaders who teach damnable doctrines, while we sit on our hands and pray about what he is teaching and believe showing "love" is going to change the outcome. Meanwhile, countless people who listen to him are being infected with a terminal disease, when we had the medicine, we knew the answer, and we knew he was wrong. But we loved our image and reputation more than the person who we pretended to love.

Holocaust survivor and Nobel Laureate Elie Wiesel said, "What hurts the victim the most is not the cruelty of the oppressor, but the silence of the bystander." And he also mentioned that, "Silence encourages the tormentor, never the tormented." When followers of the Lord give tacit approval to such leadership, it is not the love of God we are displaying. It is treason.

Before I first published *Shepherds, Hirelings, and Dictators,* I had an encounter with a well-known leader, who those within the church as well as those outside the church seeks and respects his words as if they are from God himself. This leader took it upon himself to offer me "godly" counsel and suggested that I not publish the book. He suggested that doors would open up and how financially prosperous I would be if I listened to his advice. He also mentioned that if I didn't heed his advice that it could bring a judgment upon my ministry and my income. Such advice along with other misguided comments were laughable at times, but at other times heartbreaking. It was heartbreaking that people who claimed to be saved and filled with God's Spirit would object to something that was backed by plenty of Scripture references. These were not isolated verses pulled out of their context to support my particular opinion; still, verses explained in an exegetical manner was not enough to convince some.

It baffled me how people claimed to be Spirit-filled believers but rejected the very Scriptures that the Holy Spirit wrote. And then I came to realize that many did not attack me over the Word of God—after all, how could they win? No, they attacked me because of the message. You see, as a pastor, I had broken the unwritten and unspoken rule: Do not speak against other leaders. As in corporate America and today's political arena, silence has now become a code of honor and trust in the church. In other words, you don't "sell out" your own. If you want to be promoted and welcomed into larger circles, prove your loyalty by your silence. But I have come to understand that blind loyalty is no loyalty at all; it is cowardly, duplicitous and self-serving.

In times of gross apathy and apostasy, standing on the Lord's side and standing up for his Word's sake will cause you to be labeled and viewed in a negative way, not just from the world, but from the very ones who profess that Jesus is Lord. But I take my stand with Athanasius, an Alexandrian bishop and theologian in the year 328. His year-after-year battles with other bishops and emperors over his stance on doctrinal issues caused him to be exiled five times by four different rulers for a total of more than seventeen years. If that wasn't enough, he took a hard stand against Arius, a fellow minister who taught an erroneous dogma called *Arianism*, the heretical doctrine that teaches and believes that Jesus is a created being; therefore, he and the Father could not be of the same substance. In essence, Christ the Son is not coeternal and coequal with the Father. When it seemed like a majority of the Roman Empire was moving toward Arianism, a concerned friend proclaimed, "The whole world is against you." Undismayed, Athanasius responded back in his famous words, saying, "Then it is Athanasius against the world!" His unwavering courage was on display many times, and sometimes, it must have seemed like he was fighting the battle alone. But in the end, God rewarded him for standing firmly and turned the battle in his favor. His words have turned into a famous Latin phrase: *Athanasius contra mundum*—Athanasius against the world. It is a battle cry for a heart of determination that no matter how difficult the situation may appear or how strong the opposition is against you, defend and stand on the Word of God regardless of the cost.

This has been my encouragement in the midst of a lot of unjust negativity, knowing that I have a duty to represent Christ to every man, woman and child and to be devoted to his charge over my life: "Write what you see." Therefore, my allegiance is to Christ and to his faithful people. Being trendy does not equate to trustworthiness. To hear, "Well done," is greater than having a number one book in sales only to discover that in heaven I am rejected.

Other sources of encouragement have been the many emails and comments I have received from all over the world, from uplifting words from European believers to a missionary taking the book to villages in Kenya to help leaders resist and defend against the false doctrines spreading from America to their country. I have heard that some Christian publishers were using the book as a template to measure what type of manuscripts they would receive and print. Some have even refused to print any word of faith teachings including the prosperity gospel, even though from a business perspective they could have increased their coffers by selling such books. To hear that people are taking this book along with their Bibles to examine the leadership of a new church they're visiting has been mind blowing. The phone calls of people weeping and returning back to the Lord make the book all worth it.

People are finding strength to escape the grips of a hireling or dictator and are now being properly led and fed, and that is God's way. Jeremiah chapter 3 verses 14–15 record the Lord's words: "Return, O backsliding children," says the LORD, "for I am married to you. I will take you, one from a city and two from a family, and I will bring you to Zion. And I will give you shepherds according to My heart, who will feed you with knowledge and understanding."

God's promise to those who would repent and turn back to him would be giving them leaders after his heart, who would feed them with the Word of God to remove the damage of error and restore healing in their lives. Who you follow could be an indicator of how God views you.

Last year after encountering people who were facing unbiblical manners in their churches I felt forced to go back through the book again. Hearing their stories—and how they correlated with examples in the book—was shocking. The accuracy of the book revealed to them that their new problems were actually old problems and that there was an answer for it. It also revealed to me that the message in this book was neither insignificant nor outdated—it was still alive.

Knowing this, I felt it was time for a second edition, but a revised version. Rereading some of the biblical truths I wrote about in the first edition of the book made me disheartened again because after all these years nothing has changed; in reality, it has gotten worse. Within a decade, we have seen a rise in the social media market, which has helped spread this destructive flame. We once had to be concerned about what was being preached from the pulpits, but now we have to be concerned about what is being promoted over the Internet, as well. Unbiblical and unsound leaders now have an avenue to broadcast their damnable doctrines and beliefs as they go unchecked from any spiritual correction. In this age of social media branding, those incompetent and self-appointed can create, build platforms, and draw followers even though God has not approved them.

We are living in a very dangerous time when people are governing their truths and authenticity by how many followers they have and a "like" button, but not the Scriptures.

The same destructive teachings are still around, like a deadly case of influenza, and many are still convinced these instructions are from God. For example, the first fruit offering scam is still present in many churches and on "Christian" television. A recent study discovered that about twenty percent of churchgoers in America attend a church that teaches the prosperity gospel. That is alarming. And if this is not enough, there has been an increase of devious prophets who are convincing people that they have a gift from God to attract and raise money—these false prophets claim they are "anointed" for prosperity.

## WE ARE IN A POST-TRUTH AGE

The Scripture verses that God led me to a decade ago I believe are more important now than before. In diagnosing his people's spiritual state, God speaks through the prophet Jeremiah: "A horrible and shocking thing has happened in this land—the prophets give false prophecies, and the priests rule with an iron hand. Worse yet, my people like it that way! But what will you do when the end comes?" (Jer. 5:30–31).

If there is any period of history that remarkably correlates with our present times, it is ancient Judah in the days of Jeremiah. Judah was a nation that was spiraling down quickly. It was a nation that was on the verge of something cataclysmic; but sadly, very few could see it. In essence, it was a nation that from the surface appeared prosperous, but yet was descending deeply into a moral and spiritual crisis. Delusion permeated the religious scene, while divisiveness perverted the political arena. The people were so deluded in their perspective of God that hearing a true Word from God was repulsive; therefore, they misdiagnosed their true standings with him.

Mark this down: When God's people neglect what they know to be true and then join themselves to something antithetical to God's character, the culture around them will start to decay. The culprit behind the downfall of such people was one lie and then another one and another one. Believing lies and telling lies had become normal. Does this sound familiar? The culture had become so engrained and desensitized by lies that the truth sounded like an untruth—a definition of a *post-truth age*. I speak about this more in my book, *"Warnings from the Garden: Uncovering the Wiles of Deception."* A post-truth age is a time period in which important objective facts have diminished influence in shaping one's opinion. It's an age driven by selfish ambition, self-appeasement and personal biases; one in which people are more likely to accept or believe a viewpoint based on their subjunctive emotions, rather than one based on obvious facts. The post-truth age sets the stage for perception to triumph over reality and for lies to be repeatedly spoken without consequences. After all, alternative facts are not harmful as long as they bring one to his or her desired end. It's an age of glorified dishonesty.

God had seen enough. The hour was late and in his last attempt to call off his impending judgment, he raised up Jeremiah to be the voice that proclaimed his words at 11:59 p.m. —only one minute left. God uses two strong words to describe his people's deplorable spiritual condition: *horrible and shocking*. It is one thing for us to call something horrible and shocking, but it is altogether different when the Creator uses those words. When God uses these phrases it means something has exceeded human comprehension. In other words, what was being done by his people was so horrifying and repulsive that mere words could not fully express it. The behavior of his people had surpassed humankind's mental capabilities for reasoning. And who God saw as despicable were the *prophets* who spoke falsely and pronounced prophetic words without divine inspiration from him.

### REFORMATION IS NOT THE SAME AS REVOLUTION

The increase of fraudulent prophets and their acceptance among the people of God have always been indicators that God's people are in spiritual decline and deception. These hitmen from Satan are as predatory as wild hyenas. They will increase in numbers and strength when they find prey that is gullible, lost, hurting, weak and delusional. These men and women are spiritual imposters who pretend to be working and speaking on the behalf of God, but they are hired workers on Satan's payroll. Dating back to the days that Moses warned the Israelites (Deut. 13:1–5), misleading prophets have played a significant part in times of spiritual downturns. When God's people moved backward instead of forward, it was because they listened to and believed those whom God had not approved nor sent (Jer. 14:13–16). This was one of the reasons why God raised up Jeremiah to challenge and confront these self-appointed spokesmen and to turn his people away from developing an ear for false messages. When we can freely accept and embrace a "thus says the Lord" from people God has not sent, it is a clear indication that God's people have entered into apostasy.

The second thing that God called horrible and shocking was the number of *priests ruling with an iron hand.* The priest were set apart by God to teach the people the Law—how to discern between the holy and the unholy, the clean and the unclean (Lev. 10:9–11). On the contrary, these priests were self-governed. I call it the *Diotrephes syndrome,* named after a self-centered man mentioned in 3 John 9–10. Those who were called to serve were instead desiring to be served, exercising dominion over those who didn't belong to them. The priests were leading the people by their own authority and usurping the authority of God. The priests were hungry for power and used their authority in an unethical manner. The very leaders who were commissioned to guide the people into God's presence were now leading them away from the correct path.

The final thing that God called repulsive and shocking was that after being told constant lies and treated harshly by a corrupt leadership system, *his people liked it.* In Hebrew, the word *liked* is actually the word *love.* It means something that is full, having been satisfied by a fulfilled desire. The people were fully satisfied with the wicked leadership because the deviant character of the leaders allowed them to live their lives in rebellion without any restrictions or conviction. In essence, the sins of the leaders strengthened the hands of the people to desire and pursue their own course of living free from any type of godly correction. The prophets, priests and people were all in harmony on earth, but all were clashing with the God of heaven. Just because people appear to be of the same accord does not mean that heaven is in agreement. The end does not justify the means, and neither is the majority always right. Following the crowd doesn't mean you are following the Shepherd. When leadership is defiled in God's house and the people continue to defend, seeing nothing wrong, there remains nothing else but his justifiable judgment.

Learning from church history, one cannot help but see the clear and present danger we are facing. When writing this a decade ago, I assumed deceptive teaching was largely an American problem; but I have come to find out that it is a global epidemic. Social media platforms have made it not only possible to transmit truth, it has also become the vehicle to infect countless with an eternal disease.

We are in a desperate need of a *reformation* and not a revolution. Knowing the difference between the two is paramount in discerning true legitimate voices from those who are self-ordained. *Revolution* means to overturn something or to overthrow. Its origins is rooted in the struggle of power. Take notice of this absolute: *Every person who is not sent by God will be driven by power.*

Thirst for power is one reason that these untruthful leaders assume spiritual titles and demand people to call them by those titles; such deference gives them a sense of being accepted and validates their importance. They pretend to be passionate and zealous, but power and authority are rooted in their character and sprinkled throughout their speech; thus, they do not mind reminding their church of who they are. They have no hesitation in using the name of Christ as a means to establish their own personal kingdom. They need power in order to survive.

One of the most dangerous persons you will encounter is the one who is completely incompetent but yet married to power. It's called the Dunning-Kruger effect. It's a psychological disorder that describes the way people who are the least competent at a task, frequently rate their skills as exceptionally high because they are too ignorant to know what it would mean to have the right acquired skill. The lack of self-awareness to diagnose their own ability along with subpar cognitive skills leads them to overestimate their own capabilities. In biblical terminology it's called pride; self-appointed. This person's entire identity revolves around people acknowledging his power and surrendering to that power. While having this mindset, it's easy for the impostor to embrace unscriptural and devious teachings—such as dominion theology or kingdom now theology, armor bearers, spiritual mantles and heavy shepherding theology—to support this love for power.

It is true that Christ and the Scriptures teach us to submit ourselves to leadership, but that submission is predicated on the leaders following him. Hebrews 13:17 reads, "Obey those who rule over you, and be submissive, for they watch over your souls, as those who must give account . . ." The word *rule* in the Greek means to lead, not to control. Its application is this: As your leaders are teaching and explaining the true meaning and context of the Word of God, we must obey them. Still, disingenuous leaders are skilled in finding Scriptures that seem to lend credence to what they speak of, but most of the time, they twist the original meaning in order to manipulate and strike fear in the people following. God does not look favorably upon those who seek to "lord it over" people's faith, as Paul warns in 2 Corinthians 1:24, attempting to feed themselves instead of their flocks, as Ezekiel puts it (Ezek. 34:1–3).

When I speak of reformation, I am not referring to diabolical movements such as NAR (New Apostolic Reformation). I am speaking about going backward and rediscovering the original image and purpose of something—in this case, the discovery and recovery of God's Word. Those who are truly approved by God understand that God's future is in his history, and the key to

moving forward with his Spirit is not moving on to "new" things
—it is moving back to the old (Jer. 6:16).

Every biblical prophet had this understanding of God's
history. Their assignment was to measure the current generation
in comparison to the past. The book of Jeremiah records God's
warning to people, through his prophet, about failing to listen
and follow what he proclaimed to earlier generations (Jer. 7:1–
30). The truth-telling prophets were despised and rejected. They
did not harmonize with the times. They were always out of sync
with their culture because what they proclaimed went against the
current flow. The assignment they were given was fashioned and
shaped by eternity; therefore, the message they preached was
usually frowned upon because it had a countercultural
perspective. For example, Stephen, the deacon, in the book of
Acts, was called to proclaim a message that was out of touch
with his generation (Acts 7:51–60). He was considered irrelevant
in his time but was in sync with heaven's time. He was rejected
and stoned by those who claimed they knew God, but he was
accepted and received a standing ovation from Christ. To be
accepted by heaven will cause you to be at odds with people on
earth. If heaven applauds you, this world will resist you. People
who are claiming to be sent by the Lord in these last days but
their ministries are rubbing shoulders with that which is popular
and trendy are in danger of being self-ordained and illegitimate.
Remember this: Every biblical prophet we now recognize to be
true was considered unpopular, false and irrelevant during their
lifetime.

Leonard Ravenhill, an English Christian evangelist and
author, once said, "If Jesus came back today, He wouldn't
cleanse the temple, He'd cleanse the pulpit." It is for this reason I
believe it is time to reintroduce and reissue this book. I am just
as alarmed today as I was ten years ago. My friend Bill
Muehlenberg, who leads the ministry CultureWatch in

Melbourne, Australia, recently said, "Unless we start getting biblical men in our pulpits, we will not find many real believers in our pews."

I love the church and I am a true believer of the vital role that a local assembly plays in a believer's spiritual development, but I am disturbed and offended by the ideas that continue to exist in Christ's name but are void of his character and contrary to his Word. A redefinition of love has caused us to lose our righteous indignation. Sometimes the only passion we display is against those who we feel are not supporting our goals. If we would defend the things that belong to Christ like we defend our favorite preachers, political parties and denominations, the landscape of the church would look different. But yet we have a multitude of adult wolves begetting younger wolves, circling the sheep while watchmen are asleep at their post, or worst, blind. It is time for us to wake up.

Another thing that I would like to make clear is that this book is not exclusively about focusing on leadership. Unbiblical leadership is to blame for many deviations within the church today, yet we have to realize that there is so much ungodly leadership because there is a market for it. The only reason why Saul became a king was because the people desired him. Can you imagine that the only reason why some people are known is because they are what the people wanted and not what God appointed? Frightening. The reason why Aaron built the golden the calf was because the people asked for it. A sad reality is the only reason why false leaders are strengthened and given recognition is because people who claim to know God undergird them. So it is not just the leaders at fault, it is also those who applaud and underpin them.

In order for reform to happen, three things must take place, which are what I desire to accomplish through this book:

1. Diagnosis—to reveal, announce and expose the problem;
2. Identification—to pinpoint how the problem was created;
3. Solution—to show how to come out of the problem, how to recover, and how to prevent others from the same problem.

With these goals in mind, I kept what I originally wrote, but I only added and cleaned up a few things here and there to bring better clarity. I also added a few more reasons in chapter 14 for why it is hard for some people to leave dangerous leaders and unbiblical churches, followed by sound advice on steps to recover after church hurt.

When you start to desire the truth, your intention is going to put you in direct conflict with falsehood. And when the truth is not your template, a lie will become your teacher. It is my desire to recover the truth, to reveal the truth, and to explain the truth, so you can be healed and restored by the truth.

The truth can only set you free when you have identified the lie that held you captive.

# PREFACE, 2010 EDITION

As I look out over the horizon of the body of Christ, my heart not only breaks but burns with righteous indignation. Why? The prophet Jeremiah proclaims it best: "A horrible and shocking thing has happened in this land—the prophets give false prophecies, and the priests rule with an iron hand. And worse yet, My people like it that way! But what will you do when the end comes?" (Jer. 5:30–31).

How will we respond to God's question? "Should I not punish them for this?" says the LORD. "Shall I not avenge Myself against a nation such as this?" (Jer. 5:29). Many in the body of Christ will say, "Here is another doom and gloom preacher." Call it whatever you may, but our God is a God of mercy and justice. If we have offended, manipulated and misused his name, thinking "positive thoughts" will not stop the justice of God.

For some time now, I have received frequent emails and phone calls from different believers all across America with unpleasant stories of false leaders in the church. A serious leadership issue has been developed, causing a cancer to be formed in the American church. This should not shock us because the Spirit of God has been warning us for centuries that deception and corruption in leadership shall come.

The apostle Paul said:

> "I know full well that false teachers, like vicious wolves, will come in among you after I leave, not sparing the flock. Even some of you will distort the truth in order to draw a following. Watch out! Remember the three years I was with you—my constant watch and care over you night and day, and my many tears for you" (Acts 20:29–31).

Paul's prophetic warning is the inspiration for this book. *BEWARE! The message in this book is strong, not to condemn, but to convict, recover and rebuild.* I believe the church is "primed" for another spiritual reformation—not a reformation of titles or spiritual gifts, but a returning back to biblical sound teaching. The late A. W. Tozer boldly wrote, *"Until we have a reformation, all of our books, and our schools and our magazines are only the working of bacteria in the decaying Church."* I trust this message will provoke and challenge the church to rethink what too many have assumed is from the Lord.

Several years ago, someone led me to a word given by the late Stanley Frodsham in 1965. The following is part of the prophetic word spoken to him forty-five years ago. It speaks directly to the conditions of our churches today, which is discussed throughout this book:

> *Hearken diligently concerning these things, for in the last days shall come seducing spirits that shall turn many of my anointed ones away. Many shall fall through divers' lusts, and because of sin abounding. But if you will seek me diligently I will put my Spirit within you. When one shall turn to the right hand or*

*to the left you shall not turn with them, but keep your eyes wholly on the Lord. The coming days are the most dangerous, difficult and dark, but there shall be a mighty outpouring of my Spirit upon many cities, and many shall be destroyed. My people must be diligently warned concerning the days that are ahead. Many shall turn after seducing spirits; many are already seducing my people. It is those who DO righteousness that are righteous. Many cover their sins by great theological words. But I warn you of seducing spirits who instruct my people in an evil way. Many of these I shall anoint, that they may purify and sift my people; for I would have a holy people.*

*I warn you to search the Scriptures diligently these last days. For the things that are written shall indeed be made manifest. There shall come deceivers among my people in increasing numbers, who shall speak forth the truth and shall gain the favor of the people. For the people shall examine the Scriptures and say, "What these men say is true." Then when they have gained the hearts of the people, then and THEN ONLY shall they bring out these wrong doctrines. Therefore, I say that you should not give your hearts to men, nor hold people's persons in admiration. For by these very persons shall Satan enter into my people. Watch for Seducers. Do you think a seducer will brandish a new heresy and flaunt it before the people? He will speak the words of righteousness and truth, and will appear as a minister of light, declaring the Word. The people's hearts shall be won. Then, when the hearts are won, they will bring out their doctrines, and the people shall be deceived. The people shall say, "Did he not speak thus and thus? And did we not examine it from the Word? Therefore he is a minister of righteousness. This that he has now spoken we do not see in the Word, but it must be right, for the other things he spoke were true."*

*Be not deceived. For the deceiver will first work to gain the hearts of many, and then shall bring forth his insidious doctrines. You cannot discern those who are of me and those who are not of me when they start to preach. But seek me constantly, and then when these doctrines are brought out you shall have a witness in your heart that these are not of me. Fear not, for I have warned you. Many will be deceived. But if you walk in holiness and uprightness before the Lord, your eyes shall be open and the Lord will protect you. If you will constantly look unto the Lord you will know when the doctrine changes, and will not be brought into it. If your heart is right I will keep you; and if you will look constantly to me I will uphold you.*

*The minister of righteousness shall be one this wise—his life shall agree with the Word, and his lips shall give forth that which is wholly true, and it will be no mixture. When the mixture appears then you will know he is not a minister of righteousness. The deceivers speak first the truth and then error, to cover their own sins which they love. Therefore I exhort and command you to study the Scriptures relative to seducing spirits, for this is one of the great dangers of these last days.*

*I desire you to be firmly established in my Word and not in the personalities of men that you will not be moved as so many shall be moved. I would keep you in the paths of righteousness. Take heed to yourselves and follow not the seducing spirits that are already manifesting themselves. Diligently inquire of me when you hear something that you have not seen in the Word, and do not hold people's persons in admiration, for it is by this very method that Satan will hold many of my people.*

People of God, I pray that we wake up and take serious heed to these prophetic alarms. The hour is quickly approaching for the return of our Lord and Savior Jesus Christ. For this reason, the Enemy of our souls has intensified his deception. This is the season to really distinguish a true shepherd from a false shepherd because whomever you follow in these last days will determine your end.

# INTRODUCTION

God loves mankind, and in every part of human history he did the utmost to care for his creation. Knowing we are vulnerable sheep needing protection, God has appointed shepherds over us. We call them pastors and teachers, and their role is to protect, nurture, instruct and equip the children of God. In fact, they are supposed to ultimately lead the flock of God into the Creator's very presence. But as far back as Old Testament times and up to this current age, there have been those who donned the robes and played the part but really are frauds, taking advantage of God's people for personal gain.

Throughout the generations, false prophets and insincere teachers have pretended to have the best interests of God's people in mind. They claim they are human instruments who have received direct words of the Lord through the Holy Spirit. But in the final analysis, they do *not* represent God, and they harm the sheep to the point of costing them their souls. The gospel of Matthew makes this very clear: Jesus said, "Watch out that no one deceives you. For many will come in my name, claiming, 'I am the Christ,' and will deceive many" (24:4–5).

Who are these deceitful leaders, and how can we distinguish true shepherds from wolves in shepherd's clothing? That is the question I explore in *Shepherds, Hirelings and Dictators: How to Recognize the Difference.*

Chapter 1

# BUILDING ON A FIRM FOUNDATION

THE ONLY RELIABLE FOUNDATION UPON WHICH TO BASE existence is the one that is lasting, unshakable and unfailing. This foundation is not the kind built of stone or cement, but rather it is a person—the only perfect Person who ever lived. I am referring to Jesus, the second person of the Trinity, described in Scripture as the perfect Lamb of God and the only begotten Son of God who takes away the sin of the world.

The Old Testament goes to great lengths to explain how a system of blood sacrifices was established to atone for the sins of the children of Israel. Scripture clearly says that this same system is in place in the New Testament: "In fact, the law requires that nearly everything be cleansed with blood, and without the shedding of blood there is no forgiveness" (Heb. 9:22).

The book of Leviticus details the sometimes labored and always stringent rules governing the offering of sacrifices. Leviticus 1:10 says, "And if his offering be of the flocks, namely, of the sheep, or of the goats, for a burnt sacrifice, he shall bring it a male without blemish." Every sacrifice was required to be a perfect specimen, without spot, disability or blemish of any kind in order to be accepted as a covering or expiation for sins.

The system of blood sacrifices found in the Old Testament was a type and shadow—a foretelling—of the final, perfect sacrifice that would come in time, fulfilling the promise of God. Jesus of Nazareth was the fulfillment of that promise, and because he was the only sinless person ever born, it was appointed to him to die to pay for the sins of the world. He is our perfect Lamb, the model after which every good shepherd should be patterned.

In the same way, God and his unchangeable Word must be the foundation upon which we build our personal lives. Matthew 7:26–27 talks about the wisdom of building on rock rather than sand and warns that when we build on sinking sand our building will shift and, ultimately, fall. The same is true of following after unreliable shepherds who teach other gospels and lead their people in the wrong direction. Proverbs 25:19 says, "confidence in an unfaithful man in a time of trouble is like a bad tooth or a lame foot." In other words, he will be a hindrance rather than a help in times of trial when he is needed the most. Only God is faithful and never breaks promises.

God is as solid and as reliable as his Word. He is consistent and does not change (Mal. 3:6). The Lord is the same yesterday and today and forever (Heb. 13:8). He is not fickle or moody, but rather he is steadfast and immovable, even when we are unfaithful.

Bankers are trained to recognize counterfeit money by conducting an intensive study of the real thing so that they know it when they see it. And when they are able to identify the detailed qualities of the real thing, they can spot a fake in an instant. This is exactly the way Jesus taught his disciples during his earthly ministry when he instructed them to discern and rightly divide the Word of Truth, for only then would they be able to recognize false doctrine. In Matthew 16:6, Jesus told the disciples to be on their guards: "Take heed and beware of the doctrine of the Pharisees and Sadducees."

For the protection of his people, God has given us his Holy Spirit, his infallible Word and discernment. The apostle John tells us to try the spirits to see whether they are of God: "Dear friends, do not believe every spirit, but test the spirits to see whether they are from God, because many false prophets have gone out into the world" (1 John 4:1). He defines what a false prophet is when he says, "Many deceivers, who do not acknowledge Jesus Christ as coming in the flesh, have gone out into the world" (2 John 7). John does not gives us a complete definition of a false prophet, but defines it based on the group of men that he was addressing at that time. Simply put, if shepherds do not agree that Jesus Christ has come in the flesh, they are not of God. A good tree cannot produce evil fruit, just as a bad tree cannot bear good fruit. Our task is to be discerning fruit inspectors to determine whether someone is truly from God. "Thus, by their fruit you will recognize them" (Matt. 7:20). This is the way to build on a firm foundation.

The Bible is no ordinary book. It is called *the living Word* for a reason. Hebrews 4:12 tells us, "For the word of God is living and powerful, and sharper than any two-edged sword, piercing even to the division of soul and spirit, and of joints and marrow, and is a discerner of the thoughts and intents of the heart."

The Word of God has been around for thousands of years, though evil men and even the Devil himself have tried to destroy it. It is also the only book ever written that can actually transform the heart of men and women from the inside out. This is why it must be the foundation upon which everything else is built. Any other foundation that is laid is substandard and will eventually fail. Scripture must be the standard by which everything else is measured. If a teaching does not stand up to the scrutiny of the Bible, it should be discarded, for if it is not the truth, it is a lie.

In the last days it will be more important than ever to know God intimately, to spend time in prayer, and to have the mind and heart of God. It is vital to know the Word so we are not confused when we hear questionable teachings or distortions of the gospel.

### THE PURPOSE OF THE CHURCH

The church of Jesus Christ represents the bride of Christ. The relationship is an example of the love between Jesus, the Bridegroom, and his bride, the church. Therefore, the church should not only be a place where sin-sick people go to find forgiveness, redemption and healing; it should be a place where the redeemed can regain their spiritual balance, a safe place from a world that takes advantage at every opportunity.

If the life-giving Word is preached, it will do its own work by the power of the Holy Spirit. It will transform people and help them realize that the King of Kings and Creator of the universe gave up his throne in heaven, took on the form of a man, and died in their place to redeem them from sin, hell, the grave and the clutches of Satan himself. The purpose of the church is to teach and equip so that we may be changed into new creations in Christ Jesus, reflecting the love of God to those who do not know him (2 Cor. 5:17). And the church is to prepare us to win and disciple souls, bringing them to maturity so they can go tell others of our Lord Jesus, whether they are in the marketplace, the workplace or wherever they happen to be (Matt. 28:19–20).

The church is to train Christians to be holy and passionate

about Jesus, and to function in the gifts of the Spirit with signs and wonders following so that all may grasp the truth that God is alive and well and that he loves them. The church is mandated to preach and ground people in the Word so they can give a reason for the hope that is in them. Paul said, "Preach the Word; be prepared in season and out of season; correct, rebuke and encourage—with great patience and careful instruction" (2 Tim. 4:2 NLT). The apostle Peter told us "in your hearts set apart Christ as Lord. Always be prepared to give an answer to everyone who asks you to give the reason for the hope that you have" (1 Pet. 3:15).

## GOD'S ORIGINAL INTENT

Psalm 103 says, "He made known His ways to Moses, His acts to the children of Israel" (103:7). Because Moses was well acquainted with the ways of God, he could not be deceived. God reveals himself through his Word, his will, his order and his purpose. When we talk about the ways of God, we have to start at the beginning to understand his original intent for a thing. This is why spending time in God's Word is so vital because it is only there that we can learn his original intent. Apart from spending time reading and meditating on Scripture, there is no way to know the ways of God.

There are different terms in English that can be used for *knowledge* or *understanding*. We may think we understand God because we have heard *about* him. But in God's kingdom the word *knowledge* does not only mean having intellectual information about something. Rather, it is an intimate, progressive revelation bringing about permanent and life-changing transformation in the heart.

To really grasp the truths of God we must have revelation that comes by the help of the Holy Spirit. Otherwise, we possess a mere collection of facts that, in the end, mean nothing. In truth, it is the Spirit of God who reveals and helps us understand the depth of who God is and how he operates (1 Cor. 2:7–12). Without the Spirit of God, there are only dead words. The Spirit brings life, stability, revelation, and ultimately, unparalleled fellowship with our amazing God.

Unfortunately, the purpose of the church has been misunderstood and distorted in our day. For some, it has become the place to build a career network and make business connections. These things in themselves are not bad. But when the church is functioning more like a business trade show, we have lost our focus. We have also lost our direction when the church is used as a dating service. Many relationships among brothers and sisters in Christ have been tarnished by such worldly practice.

In many places, the church has become a center for mere entertainment that draws in large followings. In such places the Bible is simply a prop, used as a resource, but not as the source; there is no true teaching or explaining the meaning of the Scriptures, just isolated verses being used to inspire "seekers" but not challenge them. What happens when seekers are placed in the hands of a worldly church? They become mere customers and not authentic worshippers. Yet worse, they are convinced they know God, and they are ready to meet Christ. They believe they are redeemed, but no true regeneration has taken place. They believe they are saved from the wrath of God, yet no sanctification has happened. They believe they are forgiven of their sins but have disregarded and downplayed biblical repentance. Jesus did not preach a gospel of forgiveness, he preached a gospel of repentance! "Repent of your sins and turn to God, for the kingdom of Heaven is near," he preached (Matt. 4:17 NLT). You cannot be forgiven of your sins until you repent; but you cannot repent unless you are convicted of your sins.

Recently, a leader over one of the largest churches in America said it is not his goal to make people feel guilty since life does that daily, because if you lay shame on the people, they will get turned off and leave. Well, I assume Jesus didn't get that memo—he taught in such a way that many of his disciples walked away and he turned to the Twelve that were handpicked by him and asked if they wanted to go, as well (John 6:60–71). In other places, there are those who use the church for the purpose of soliciting money. When the church becomes a safe haven for people to practice extortion without being caught, the proper response to these so-called leaders is to remember Jesus' righteous anger when he cleansed the temple in the second chapter of the gospel of John (13–17).

The church has lost so much of its original intent that it is scarcely recognizable as the body of Christ. It is common these days to see divisions, factions, criticism, power-struggles, arguments, strife, jealousy and competition between brothers and sisters in Christ. How tragic is this? Jesus told us to "Love one another. As I have loved you, so you must love one another. By this all men will know that you are my disciples, if you love one another" (John 13:34–35). If the only way for the world to see Christ is by looking at Christians and the church, what a long way we have fallen.

It was never God's intention for the church to function like a business in corporate America, nor was it ever intended as a depot for finding a mate. People who attend church for such reasons are deceived. In fact, we might want to inspect their fruit to see if they really know God at all. It is a sad truth that just because someone goes to church, or quotes Scripture backward and forward, or sings all the songs and go through all the motions, does not mean he or she is a genuine Christian believer! It should sober us to realize that the Devil can quote Scripture as well as the most learned Christian scholars (Luke 4:9–11). The only difference is that he uses it to manipulate and deceive others. The same is true of unfaithful shepherds.

As the body of Christ, we open ourselves to this kind of deception when we operate in our flesh rather than submitting to God in all areas of our lives. To protect ourselves, it would be wise to make sure what we are taught lines up with God's Word.

Chapter 2

# DO NOT BE DECEIVED

THEN JESUS WENT OUT AND DEPARTED FROM THE TEMPLE, AND His disciples came up to show Him the buildings of the temple. And Jesus said to them, "Do you not see all these things? Assuredly, I say to you, not one stone shall be left here upon another—that shall not be thrown down." Now as He sat on the Mount of Olives, the disciples came to Him privately, saying, "Tell us, when will these things be? And what will be the sign of Your coming and the end of the age?" And Jesus answered and said to them: "Take heed that no one deceives you. For many will come in My name, saying, 'I am the Christ,' and will deceive many" (Matt. 24:1–5).

Jesus was about to fulfill prophecy. Recognizing that he had only a few days left on earth before he would be crucified, he went to the temple and made a statement to the Pharisees. He said he would leave their house desolate (Matt. 23:38). In other words, whatever they had built would be torn down. Not long afterward, the disciples asked Jesus if he had seen the beautiful buildings, one of which was a temple trimmed in gold and precious gems and built by Herod. Because they knew how terribly labor-intensive the temple was, they were astonished to hear him say a day would come when it would be torn down. In essence, the Lord was warning them not to be taken in by appearances. What looks good on the outside can be deceiving. He had spoken of whitewashed tombs, "which look beautiful on the outside but on the inside are full of dead men's bones and everything unclean" (Matt. 23:27).

As they walked toward the Mount of Olives, Jesus began teaching them the sign of his coming and of the end of the age (technically, eschatology, or the study of last things). Last things are very important because they include warnings, signs and milestones that signify Christ's return is very near.

### THE SIGNS OF HIS COMING

So often teachers only mention a single sign of the last days —wars and rumors of wars. But that was not the first or only sign Jesus mentioned. He also spoke of the destruction of the temple and of an increase in deception. And while deception did occur in Jesus' day, he warned that deception would greatly intensify as his return drew near.

It was at that point Jesus turned to the leaders who would be responsible for preaching the gospel, and it was to them that he directed comments about deception. It is vital to clarify that the Lord was not talking about an increase in radical Muslim influence, or about persecution by other unbelievers. Neither was he referring to those who would reject Jesus as the Son of God. As surprising as it sounds, he was referring to a deception taking place among Christians right within his own church.

He turned to address the disciples and said, "Take heed that no one deceives you! For many will come in My name, saying, 'I am the Christ,' and will deceive many."

Many Christians have interpreted this passage to mean we should watch out for those who come claiming to be the Christ, *the anointed one.* But what Jesus meant was that many will come in Christ's name, *not with his name*, alleging they have been anointed to represent him and speak on his behalf. In other words, "The Lord told me to tell you" or "The Lord spoke this to me." "The Lord gave me this revelation" or "The Lord called me to do this." (Many claim "the Lord called me to do this" even when the calling is contrary to the Word of God. Jesus will never call anyone to do anything that goes against Scripture.)

Jesus said many would follow after those who claim to represent him when he never sent them or approved of them. Here is the really alarming thing: In the Greek, the word *many* means more than, plenteous and majority; in fact, it describes a number so great that it cannot be numbered. Following after such false teachers will only lead us into trouble and entanglement. Scripture says that if the blind lead the blind, both will fall into a pit or ditch (Matt. 15:14). In this case, however, the ditch refers to eternal separation from God.

## God Is Breaking His Silence and the Verdict Is in

In the last days, God will speak out and bring many things out of the closet. Up until now, he has been observing the church in silence. But now he has finished deliberating and is about to render his verdict. As a body of Christ, we have been taking God's silence as approval and tolerance of our conduct and teachings. But his silence does not imply this at all. His silence signifies a soon judgment: "These things you have done and I kept silent; you thought I was altogether like you. But I will rebuke you and accuse you to your face" (Ps. 50:21). Once God has made the transition from observation mode to recompense mode, people will be rewarded for their work, whether good or bad. Scripture says judgment is at the door: "For the time has come for judgment to begin at the house of God, and if it begins with us first, what will be the end of those who do not obey the gospel of God? Now if the righteous one is scarcely saved, where will the ungodly and the sinner appear?" (1 Pet. 4:17–18).

The word *judgment* strikes fear in our hearts, but it simply means Almighty God is about to make a decision based on his investigation. It should not bother us unless we have walked away from the truth and rebelled against God. Remember the story of the Patriarch Abraham? God came to earth with two angels, trying to decide whether or not to tell Abraham everything despite that someday he would be the father of a great nation (Gen. 18:1–35). During that interaction, God told Abraham that one of the reasons he came down was to see if what he heard about Sodom and Gomorrah was really true. When he learned that it was so, God rendered his verdict and brought judgment down on both. But because Abraham prayed and asked God to spare his nephew Lot, a resident of that evil city, God employed angels to physically remove his loved ones in the nick of time.

God loves his people and always warns them when it is time to move on. Perhaps he is trying to warn us that it is time to move out of unfaithful churches because judgment is coming. Why would God be releasing this word now? Because there are still many righteous ones sitting under the teaching of hirelings and dictators. Many of these churches are going to close and stop broadcasting over radio and television due to lack of support. In effect, God will close them because they were a "vision" of man rather than a revelation from God.

The question we must ask then is this: If God so loves his people, why does he allow harmful leaders into the church to deceive Christians in the first place? While this issue might cause confusion, it fits completely with the character of God, who always warns his people so they are equipped to make wise choices. True love will always warn beforehand. This has been true all the way back to the Garden of Eden, when God warned Adam beforehand: "You are free to eat from any tree in the garden; but you must not eat from the tree of the knowledge of good and evil, for when you eat of it you will surely die" (Gen. 2:16–17).

When the disciples asked Jesus to tell them what would be the signs of his coming and the end of the age, he answered them by saying, "Take heed that no one deceives you. For many will come in My name, saying, 'I am the Christ,' and will deceive many." He is warning us of what is to come, once again equipping the church for every good thing. If we are listening, we will wisely heed the warnings about false shepherds and how to identify them.

Chapter 3

# FOUNDATIONAL FAITH

IN RECENT YEARS WE HAVE HEARD A GREAT DEAL OF PREACHING about faith, and it has often brought about confusion. This is because the topic of faith has been misused and distorted.

What is faith? The writer of the Epistle to the Hebrews says it is "the substance of things hoped for, the evidence of things not seen" (Heb. 11:1). This is true, but this is more of a description and not the definition of faith. The definition of faith is trust in God in all circumstances. This view of faith enables believers to persevere and remain loyal to God and his Word at all times.

The important thing to remember is the foundation our faith is built upon. There is a broad sense of faith. For example, both Muslims and Buddhists have faith. In the case of a Christian (one who has a personal relationship with Jesus Christ), faith rests in Christ and comes by hearing the Word of God that attests to his faithfulness. *A Christian chooses to take God at his Word, believing what he has said.*

If we spend time with the Lord we can know him intimately and even understand exactly how he thinks, including what he loves and hates. Romans 12:2 says to be "transformed by the renewing of your minds, that you may prove what is that good and acceptable and perfect will of God." That is what it means when saying believers have the mind of Christ. These things, then, form the firm foundation upon which a child of God can stake his or her life.

Truly, God has given us everything we need to overcome the world, the flesh and the Devil. God's very DNA dwells in the Holy Spirit who dwells inside us. Now that is something to get excited about! Therefore, whatever we need to defeat the enemy is already at our disposal. We must first believe, put on the full armor of God (Eph. 6:13), and stand against the wiles of the evil one instead of falling on our swords in defeat.

The Father's very glory indwells us. He created us with bodies that are miraculous in their design. He gave us brothers and sisters of like Christian faith so we would never live in isolation. When Adam and Eve sinned, he already had a plan in place, circumventing the Enemy's plot to destroy us for good. He loved us when we were anything but lovable, and he died to redeem us from sin, death and eternal separation. Then he made plans to spend personal time alone with us because he loves fellowship and wants a close relationship with each of us. God is never distracted; he actually inclines his ear to hear our prayers (Psalm 40:1–3). His line is never busy, nor does he tell us to "press one for more options." Christ is there for us twenty-four/seven, promising never to leave nor forsake us (Heb. 13:5). Knowing these things should blow us away. In the same way, God wants us to develop and use our talents to bless others. He wants us to use what we possess to establish the kingdom. This should be the goal of every good shepherd.

## THE ATTITUDE OF A GOOD SHEPHERD

Many may have their own view on what they perceive a

good shepherd to be. But a good shepherd is really one with a tender compassion toward the sheep and does what is best for the sheep in light of eternity. In the second chapter of First Corinthians, Paul talks about his feelings on being a shepherd:

> "And I, brethren, when I came to you, did not come with excellence of speech or of wisdom declaring to you the testimony of God. For I determined not to know anything among you except Jesus Christ and Him crucified. I was with you in weakness, in fear, and in much trembling, and my speech and my preaching were not with persuasive words of human wisdom, but in demonstration of the Spirit and of power, that your faith should not be in the wisdom of men, but in the power of God. . . . But God has revealed them to us through His Spirit. For the Spirit searches all things, yes, the deep things of the spirit. . . . But the natural man does not receive the things of the Spirit of God, for they are foolishness to him; nor can he know them, because they are spiritually discerned" (1–5; 10; 14).

God gives us life and uses us as instruments to speak the words of healing and restoration that bring about a change of heart. Not just anyone can be used by God, for he handpicks those who are humble and draw near to him, and authorizes those who recognize that he is the only source of life.

Paul is a good example of such a shepherd. He understood his role of a spiritual leader, yet he humbly preached with fear and trembling, knowing God would not hold him blameless should he mislead his people.

## COULD YOUR PASTOR HAVE WRITTEN THIS LETTER?

Paul shared his desires and the potential he saw for the growth and spiritual maturity of the church:

> "To the church of God which is at Corinth, to those who are sanctified in Christ Jesus, called to be saints, with all who in every place call on the name of Jesus Christ our Lord, both theirs and ours. Grace to you and peace from God our Father and the Lord Jesus Christ. I thank my God always concerning you for the grace of God which was given to you by Christ Jesus, that you were enriched in everything by Him in all utterance and all knowledge, even as the testimony of Christ was confirmed in you, so that you come short in no gift, eagerly waiting for the revelation of our Lord Jesus Christ, who will also confirm you to the end, that you may be blameless in the day of our Lord Jesus Christ" (1 Cor. 1:2–8).

A pastor who could have written this letter is a good shepherd. There is encouragement in Paul's tone. There is excitement in his heart and confidence in his voice as he urges the Corinthians on toward godliness. A good shepherd will respect his sheep and trust God to work in them at all times. He will speak uplifting words of heartfelt and sincere blessing—not empty words of flattery. He does not shy away from the hard truths that demand repetition, for the human nature has a tendency to believe repackaged lies. He understands that he has been mandated by Christ to preach the things that are proper for sound doctrine, knowing that only sound teaching applied can bring forth sound living (1 Tim. 4:16; Titus 2:1). If your pastor does not have this kind of attitude toward you and others in your congregation, is it time to find someone else who will?

## THE ORDER OF GOD

Before God manifests a promise, he will first bring his people into the proper order of things. In other words, before the Master does anything new in our lives, he will first bring us back to his original order so we can have a solid starting place from which to move. When Jesus was released into his ministry, God had already sent a forerunner named John the Baptist. John's sole purpose was to prepare the way for Christ by bringing the Jewish nation to a place of repentance and re-establishing their relationship with the Father. John's mission was significant because the scribes and Pharisees had succeeded in twisting and devaluing God's Word, causing it to lose its original intent.

The religious system of John's day had been around for a very long time, but it was still wrong. Just because something has been around a long time does not mean it is of God—even if it started out right. The Father brought the Son onto the scene to restore the order that had been lost, to restore life to a dead system of religion. But he did not merely dust it off and clean it up; he transformed it by actually upsetting the status quo and turning the world upside down. He confounded people's logic at every turn to the point that the religious leaders of that day felt Jesus was a threat to their system and plotted how they might kill him (Mark 3: 6).

During Jesus' day Herod was king, but in reality his reign was illegal. According to Bible history, the king of Israel was to come out of the tribe of Jacob, not the tribe of Esau (Gen. 27:28–29). Herod, however, was an Edomite, of the lineage of Esau. In Romans 9:13, we read about whom God chose and whom he rejected: "As it is written, 'Jacob have I loved, but Esau have I hated.'" It is very clear that God planned for the promise to come through Jacob, and it was Jacob's family line that God intended to rule. When Jesus appeared on the scene, the kingship had been handed down to a descendant of Esau's line, who cared nothing about God or living according to godly principles. And though there were still those who lived in faith, it was time for a change.

The scribes and Pharisees of Jesus' day dedicated all their time studying the law. They knew the Scriptures by heart, but ironically they could not recognize the Messiah when he arrived (John 5:39–43). They knew Scripture in the same way it is possible for us to know it, inside out and upside down, and still did not know God on a personal level. There are highly regarded seminary professors with all kinds of initials behind their names who do not have a personal relationship with Christ. They know a multitude of facts about Jesus and his life, but they are not intimately acquainted with our living Lord. They do not know him. And that may sound surprising, being that so many of us assume those who know much must be personally acquainted with the Source.

It is still God's intention to confound the world with the simplicity of the gospel of Christ. In these final days we must get back to the basics. We must be holy, yearning for the presence of God, preparing our hearts so he will reveal himself and move among us to establish his kingdom.

We need to press in to the secret place of God so we can know him, because without fellowship we are subject to deception and we are vulnerable to the lies of the Enemy. Because something seems to work and even makes sense does not mean it is of God. Because someone has a huge following does not mean they are anointed (consider Simon the Sorcerer in Acts 8:9–10). It is time to start measuring what we see with what God's Word says and let our hearts be led by the Holy Spirit.

According to 2 Timothy 4:2, true leaders are to "preach the Word of God. Be persistent, whether the time is favorable or not. Patiently correct, rebuke, and encourage the people with good teaching" (NLT). They are to speak the truth in love and teach doctrinal concepts, including propitiation, the conviction of the

Holy Spirit, sin, righteousness, judgment and repentance. They need to model holiness and wisdom, do good works and show love and forgiveness. They must rightly divide the Word of Truth, encouraging their people to love God with all their hearts, souls, minds and strength. They must teach them to discern between the clean and the unclean, deny themselves and pick up their cross and follow him daily. Where do we hear that kind of preaching anymore?

Paul's first letter to Timothy is truly the perfect handbook for leaders. When the apostle wrote it, he knew Timothy felt young and ill-equipped for the job of traveling and ministering on the road with him, and yet Paul encouraged him to know God's Word and live it out in the trenches. Paul set out this definition of what an elder should be:

> "So a church leader must be a man whose life is above reproach. He must be faithful to his wife. He must exercise self-control, live wisely, and have a good reputation. He must enjoy having guests in his home, and he must be able to teach. He must not be a heavy drinker or be violent. He must be gentle, not quarrelsome, and not love money. He must manage his own family well, having children who respect and obey him. For if a man cannot manage his own household, how can he take care of God's church? A church leader must not be a new believer, because he might become proud, and the devil would cause him to fall. Also, people outside the church must speak well of him so that he will not be disgraced and fall into the devil's trap (3:2–7 NLT).

This is not an exhaustive list of the character traits a leader must exhibit. We can assume that Paul also meant a leader should be free of addictions and a man of integrity in every way. True shepherds will never add to or take away from the Word of

God, "the whole counsel or God," in other words, all that God wants the flock to know (Acts 20:27), nor will they ever minimize directives God takes seriously. And true shepherds will never wink at sin. Rather, they will seek the wisdom of God in every situation and confront tough issues that may, in the end, cost sheep their souls.

The goal of a godly shepherd should be the ultimate health and well-being of the sheep, equipping them to rightly divide the Word of Truth. The welfare of those in his charge includes the spiritual, emotional and physical (in that order). To that end, he will speak words of life and envision the sheep as coming to maturity and wholeness in Christ, knowing that the Holy Spirit will do the work of maturing them in God's time. And while a pastor is patient as they are growing, he also knows that God is not satisfied letting them remain immature: "Brothers, stop thinking like children. In regard to evil be infants, but in your thinking be adults" (1 Cor. 14:20).

A good shepherd teaches the whole counsel of God in the context in which it was written. He does not water it down to make it more palatable, or change it to suit his hearers to win a popularity contest. Rather he shares the Word as it is in its entirety and allows God to be responsible for the outcome. God instructed the prophet Jeremiah by commanding him to, "Tell them everything I command you; do not omit a word. Perhaps they will listen and each will turn from his evil way. Then I will relent and not bring on them the disaster I was planning because of the evil they have done" (26:2–3). The good shepherd does what God says; he does not worry about whether people are offended (Mark 15:12–14). The truth is that the Word is, in itself, an offense to people who refuse to hear and repent. In fact, no one comes to God unless God has enabled him or her (John 6:60–68).

And while a laborer is worthy of his wages (1 Tim. 5:17–19), a true leader does not use his pastoral authority to line his pockets. Like Jesus, he should have a hand open to God, knowing God loves generosity and promises to meet his needs.

Many pastors start out on fire for God, obeying the leading of the Spirit, and yet somewhere along the line they begin focusing on the technical process of leadership rather than on God himself. They begin applying a corporate success model to the church as if it is merely another business to run. When a shepherd takes his eyes off Jesus, problems are inevitable, because God is no longer the center of attention. And when one's focus changes, one's preaching also subtly changes. *This is the beginning of compromise, and the slide down the slippery slope into false doctrine.*

To stay on track, those in leadership positions are wise if they examine their hearts daily to see who is on the throne of their lives. They should frequently remind themselves of what they have been rescued from, and they should cultivate an attitude of gratitude and servanthood so as never to grow cold toward God. They need to remember that he who exalts himself will be humbled, while God will exalt the one who humbles himself (Matt. 23:11–12).

It is easy to grow apathetic and bored when we have heard the gospel for years, as if it is old news. But Christ's gospel of grace is truly a cause for great excitement. It should bring us to tears when we survey the wondrous cross and realize it should have been us hanging there. And when we do get apathetic and lose interest in spiritual things, it is the job of a shepherd to warn those going in the wrong direction. The shepherd warns of dangers and snares in the road ahead, just as Ezekiel did when he was a watchman for the house of Israel (Ezek. 33:1–6). He is to equip them to hear directly from the mouth of God, so that when the shepherd is not around, the sheep are able to exercise wisdom to keep from falling into deception, and attain to the whole measure of the fullness of Christ (Eph. 4:11–13).

Even pastors who truly have a heart after God may tend to get discouraged and judge their own ministries by the size of their congregations or the amount in the offering plate. But these things are not indicators of success. Rather, success should be measured by the increasing maturity of the people and by whether or not they are growing more passionate about Jesus. It is measured by whether Christians are out there touching lives, praying for people, and winning others to Christ. It is measured by people turning from the power of Satan to the power of God.

In fact, for a church to have "great success" (as the world sees it) often means the church leader is tickling ears to pump up attendance for the purpose of increasing the church's (pastor's) treasury. If that is the reason a church is growing, God's Spirit will eventually leave and write *Ichabod*, meaning *the Lord has departed*, over the doorpost. To pump up attendance and increase the coffers, many pastors preach a broad-way gospel. But the faithful shepherd will lead congregants in the narrow way to avoid doing what is popular, no matter how tempting that may be. The road to destruction is broad, but the road to life is narrow (Matt. 7:13–14).

It would be interesting to note how often pastors begin changing their teaching out of desperation brought on by pressure. Instead of understanding it is God's problem to fix, not theirs, they do what seems "right in their own eyes" and veer off the narrow way. One does not have to read very far in the New Testament to see that Jesus always went the narrow way and against the tide of public opinion. He wasn't there to please people; he was there to change them. He is in the people-changing business to this day.

Chapter 4

# WHAT IS A SHEPHERD?

A DICTIONARY DEFINITION OF *SHEPHERD* IS (1) (N.) A PERSON who tends sheep; (2) a pastor; (3) (v.) to tend as a shepherd; and, (4) to guide or guard in the manner of a shepherd.

A shepherd is any true spiritual leader (not just a pastor, but a teacher, evangelist, prophet or apostle) who has been entrusted with the responsibility to feed, protect and nurture God's people. Some churches call them "bishops," but whatever we call them, they are the overseers of God's flock. And though we might have been led to believe otherwise, no title (function) means one person is more anointed than another.

Feeding, protecting and nurturing the flock are all equally important. A pastor cannot be an effective spiritual leader if he is always feeding but failing to protect the flock. Neither is he effective if he always protects but fails to feed his sheep. The flock will suffer if he is always nurturing, counseling and encouraging, but failing to wisely instruct and equip.

For God wanted them to know that the riches and glory of Christ are for you Gentiles, too. And this is the secret: Christ lives in you. This gives you assurance of sharing his glory. So we tell others about Christ, warning everyone and teaching everyone with all the wisdom God has given us. We want to present them to God, perfect in their relationship to Christ. That's why I work and struggle so hard, depending on Christ's mighty power that works within me (Col. 1:27–29).

Isaiah describes Christ as the perfect model of a good shepherd: "And He will feed His flock like a shepherd; He will gather the lambs with His arm, and carry them in His bosom, and gently lead those who are with young (Isa. 40:11).

God loves the sheep and will do everything in his power to see to their welfare. Scripture says the Good Shepherd lay down his life for the sheep because he loves them. He protects them even to the death (John 10:11). And that is what shepherds do. In the seventeenth chapter of First Samuel, we find the story of King David, who, as a child, shepherded his father's sheep and risked his life protecting them: "Your servant has been keeping his father's sheep. When a lion or a bear came and carried off a sheep from the flock, I went after it, struck it and rescued the sheep from its mouth. When it turned on me, I seized it by its hair, struck it and killed it" (34–35).

It is unfortunate, but leaders are prone to sin, as we all are. But they have a mandate from God, and if they take the position of pastor or teacher they must realize they are held to a higher standard of conduct and face a stricter judgment if they misuse their position (James 3:1).

In 1 Timothy chapter 3, Paul lists the character qualities of one called by God to be a shepherd. One of the requirements is that he must not be a novice or be spiritually immature. Spiritual maturity does not exclusively refer to age or length of time one has been a Christian; rather, spiritual maturity is when one walks in the likeness of Christ, exhibits self-control, and has the ability to discern truth from error and good from evil (Heb. 5:14).

In order to mature in the Christian walk, believers need a balance of preaching, teaching and warning. If any of these elements are lacking, the result is an imbalance, often opening the flock to dubious teaching and confusion. This is why Paul continually stressed sound doctrine in his epistles because sound doctrine alone produces sound living.

## SIGNS THAT IDENTIFY TRUE SHEPHERDS

- True shepherds always point people to Christ and never to themselves.
- True shepherds fear the Lord in the sense that they hold deep reverence for him. They know that any effort to lead the sheep astray will bring judgment. Because they take seriously their responsibility, they make certain that his people are properly instructed.
- True shepherds understand that the people sitting under their teaching do not belong to them but to God.
- True shepherds always encourage their people to study the Word for themselves rather than taking their word for it.
- True shepherds always make it their goal to promote the character of Christ instead of exalting their own gifts or callings.
- True shepherds never force anyone to serve in the church, but they allow God to call believers into service in his own time.
- True shepherds do not focus on being served because they understand that their calling is to serve.
- True shepherds are not egocentric. They recognize that their calling is not about them, or about their

opinions and preferences, but about serving the Lord and exalting him in all they do and say.

- True shepherds do not show partiality or favoritism.
- True shepherds feed the flock a steady diet of sound doctrine. They are responsible teachers who lead the sheep into good pasture and watch over them as they eat at their own pace.

## THE WHOLE COUNSEL OF GOD

A friend of mine shared her story with me:

"After suffering from abuse under the hand of a church dictator, my family moved to what I call a "hospital church," one whose pastor was gentle and used God's Word to encourage rather than tear down the people. His gentle ministrations were like a balm, an ointment on my open wounds that in time restored me to a place where I could once again feel God's love for me. Because of that wise shepherd's tender care, I have been healed, and have once again recovered my spiritual and emotional equilibrium."

The measure of a good shepherd then is his willingness to teach the whole counsel of God and point followers to Christ in every situation. The importance of a shepherd's influence cannot be overemphasized, because in these last days, a person's destiny will pretty much be determined by whom he or she follows. If one follows a blind man, they will both fall into a pit (Matt. 15:14). But if one follows a good shepherd who teaches the truth of God's Word without apology or excuse, that person will know the truth, know the Word and be equipped to discern truth from error.

There is no better time than now to take stock of our churches and our shepherds and compare what is done and said to God's Word. Because God loves us, he wants us to be led by faithful shepherds. We need to ask the Lord of the harvest to send out these kinds of pastors and workers (Matt. 9:35–38).

Chapter 5

# THE UNFAITHFUL SHEPHERD

To look at the subject of unfaithful shepherds, let us first consider what God says about spiritual leadership in general. The first thing to say is that spiritual leadership is very important to God. Spiritual leaders are responsible for leading the people in the direction of God and promoting the character and doctrine of Christ. Therefore, the Enemy seeks to subvert Christians and their leaders by moving them away from the whole counsel of God. Sometimes he does this by sneaking into the church through leadership (Jude 4). He knows that if the leader detours, then so will the people. The body always follows where the head leads, so wherever the leader goes, the congregation will follow. That is why Paul constantly warned believers to beware of evil men who would infiltrate the church —not just among the congregation but also among the leadership. Paul told us to be on guard against this: "I know that after I leave," he said to the Ephesian elders, "savage wolves will come in among you and will not spare the flock. Even from your own number men will arise and distort the truth in order to draw away disciples" (Acts 20:29–30).

Proverbs 29:12 says, "If a ruler is overtaken by lies, all his servants will become wicked." In other words, if a leader is influenced by a seducing spirit, everyone who follows that leader will also be misled. No matter how sincere we are or how much we love God, if we sit under the teaching of one deceived by the Enemy, we will be deceived, as well. And while we may not be sucked in by everything he does or says, we will definitely feel the impact.

There is a certain spirit behind every church leader. The spirit is either of God or not. First John 4:6 states, "whoever knows God listens to us; but whoever is not from God does not listen to us. This is how we recognize the Spirit of truth and the spirit of falsehood." When a church leader speaks, he is either led by God (the Spirit of truth) or by a seducing spirit (the spirit of error). It is up to us to discern which spirit is which, as Jesus has equipped us to do. In John 10:4–5, Jesus says, "his sheep follow him because they know his voice. But they will never follow a stranger."

Anytime we follow someone God has not truly ordained, we must check to insure that we really belong to him. If true sheep will not follow a stranger, what does that say about us if we knowingly sit under the leadership of false teachers? The word *stranger* refers to someone who is illegitimate or illegal. Perhaps this person is someone naturally gifted and charming, but they are not approved by God because they preach a distortion of the gospel.

Jesus uses the term *good shepherd* to refer to his leadership. Strangers are those who represent illegitimate leadership. He is saying that true sheep will follow him while unfaithful sheep will follow self-appointed shepherds. Therefore, who we follow is an indicator of who we belong to.

Some of us are not always aware of incorrect teaching, perhaps because it takes time to discern when teaching is off the mark. But God, in his mercy, will begin to shine the light on things done in darkness, as Jesus says in Luke 8:17.

One example of an unreliable shepherd was given by a friend:

> "We once joined a church after attending for several weeks and checking out the church's constitution and bylaws, and during that time the preaching was sound. However, within a few weeks the pastor preached from the pulpit that there was no original sin. As you can imagine, we were astounded because the Bible teaches original sin, and it is such a foundational gospel truth. Upon further investigation we learned that the pastor and his wife had recently lost a newborn, which had dramatically changed his doctrine. We had no choice, at that point, but to relinquish our membership and leave the church."

### DISCERNING FALSE TEACHING

Because God desires for us to know his truth, he will open our eyes to discern distorted teaching and lead us away from such leadership that has come under the influence of a seducing spirit. In fact, he will warn us in time to free ourselves, and then he will restore us with truth and bring us back to his original intent.

The believer who truly loves God will feel a witness in his or her spirit upon hearing false teaching, and this witness will cause them to ask God to help determine what is really happening. During this process, a Christian sitting under dubious teaching may say, "Am I crazy, or did I really just hear what I thought I heard?" And if the believer did hear correctly, one has to wonder why everyone is not as upset as he or she is. It can feel much like a *Twilight Zone* experience. However, when the truth is revealed, that Christ-follower must back away and refuse to continue sitting under false doctrine.

Some feel as if they are being disloyal to challenge or even gently question the teachings of a pastor or teacher. Others have been, in no uncertain terms, warned off, as if those in leadership are accountable to no one.

When comparing the shepherd-sheep relationship to a marriage, both are ordained by God. But nowhere does Scripture demand a wife to accept abuse. As a victim, she may have been brainwashed into believing that things are the way they were meant to be or that she is unworthy of anyone better, but that is not true. Abuse is always wrong. It is never okay, no matter who is doing it. And in the same way God has set up qualifications for a shepherd. He will remove his people from the care of a teacher who victimizes or leads his sheep astray.

If someone cannot bring themselves to leave a disqualified teacher or is constantly drawn toward them, there is something intrinsically stunted in their spiritual development; some essential building blocks are missing. Either that or the individual has never actually been redeemed. These things are true of the many people who endure erroneous teaching and even spiritual abuse week after week, unaware that such leadership is not of God.

While on this note, I think it is important to define *spiritual abuse*. The phrase has been a buzzword among believers lately; therefore, I think a proper definition is needed to ward off unjust criticism. Spiritual abuse is the misuse of one's position of power, influence and oversight to promote the self-centered desires or interests of someone other than the individual who is relying on the help. It is when one is not functioning as a leader who serves, but instead uses his authority to lord it over others and to foster and defend his own personal vision or needs (3 John 9–11). Spiritual leadership was cultivated in the heart of

God for our welfare. He did not ordain leaders so they could take advantage of his people, nor does he ever approve of such tactics.

The third chapter of the book of Micah pronounces judgment on false shepherds:

"I said, 'Listen, you leaders of Israel! You are supposed to know right from wrong, but you are the very ones who hate good and love evil. You skin my people alive and tear the flesh from their bones. Yes, you eat my people's flesh, strip off their skin, and break their bones. You chop them up like meat for the cooking pot. Then you beg the Lord for help in times of trouble! Do you really expect him to answer? After all the evil you have done, he won't even look at you! This is what the Lord says: "You false prophets are leading my people astray! You promise peace for those who give you food, but you declare war on those who refuse to feed you. Now the night will close around you, cutting off all your visions. Darkness will cover you, putting an end to your predictions. The sun will set for you prophets, and your day will come to an end. Then you seers will be put to shame, and you fortune-tellers will be disgraced. And you will cover your faces because there is no answer from God." But as for me, I am filled with power— with the Spirit of the Lord. I am filled with justice and strength to boldly declare Israel's sin and rebellion. Listen to me, you leaders of Israel! You hate justice and twist all that is right. You are building Jerusalem on a foundation of murder and corruption. You rulers make decisions based on bribes; you priests teach God's laws only for a price; you prophets won't prophesy unless you are paid. Yet all of you claim to depend on the Lord. "No harm can come to us," you say, "for the Lord is here among us." Because of you, Mount Zion will be plowed like an open field; Jerusalem will be reduced to ruins! A thicket will grow on the heights where the Temple now stands'" (3:1–12 NLT).

Does hating good and loving evil, leading people astray with false teaching, or despising justice and distorting all that is right sound like your favorite preacher? Does speaking great words of well-being to those who give the most money, but condemning and threatening those who don't give sound familiar? Does this person sound like a pastor or teacher at a church you frequently attend? Does your church have a "preach-for-pay" mentality? In other words, in everything the leader does he attaches an offering to it? If so, it is time for you to relinquish your membership because clearly there is little that can compare with the judgment of God on treacherous teachers.

Chapter 6

# WHAT IS A HIRELING?

A *HIRELING* CONNOTES SOMEONE HIRED TO DO A JOB OR PERFORM a service, usually for mercenary motives. The problem arises when someone is hired to do the job of a pastor, which requires compassion and a servant's heart. The harsh reality is that it is impossible to make someone care about people, no matter how high the pay. If the hireling feels the payoff for their service is too low, that hireling will begin to cheat, steal, manipulate, and even strong arm, because the care-factor, otherwise known as *agape love—a devoted love that results in the act of the will and not the emotions*—is tragically missing.

## SIGNS THAT IDENTIFY HIRELINGS

- Hirelings do everything for money.
- Hirelings preach and teach almost exclusively on giving.
- Hirelings twist God's Word to benefit themselves. The only reason they want others to be blessed is so that they can be blessed in return.

- Hirelings always encourage people to "sow a seed." Although they may say one cannot buy miracles, they teach that your seed is a point of contact for a miracle. Television and radio hirelings ask us to call toll-free numbers. Of course they do not mention that our name is then added to a mailing list, which they then sell to others. Soon they send out constant dunning mailings begging for money, making us feel they are desperate. Eventually, they will ask us to send our best "seed" gift to plant in "good ground," which (make no mistake about it), means their ministry rather than anyone else's.

- Hirelings sell trinkets as "points of contact." They sell all kinds of trifles—holy water, holy oil, blood of "Jesus" oil, handkerchiefs and so much more. There seems to be no limit to their imaginations when it comes to hoodwinking followers. To build credibility, they might even claim it's legitimate to believe in handkerchiefs, because after all, the garments that came off the body of Paul healed people (Acts 19:11–12). While on this note, it's important to understand what verse 11 says in this passage. It says, "Now God worked unusual miracles by the hands of Paul." The word *unusual* is also translated as special. When you properly exegete (to draw true meaning out of the text), you discover that the word unusual means this particular method for miracles were not common; it was something that God was working exclusively through the hands of Paul. Therefore, these miracles cannot be preached or believed to be something that's done again or often. If something is unusual it cannot be taught as a principle or practice. In actuality, these things are all lies and gimmicks.

- Hirelings spend great amounts of time taking up offerings.
- Hirelings claim that they are "anointed" and that God has chosen them for prosperity.

## THE TRUTH ABOUT TRINKETS

Trinkets are all about mind games, which God clearly says are perversions. People buy and carry trinkets as if they are good luck charms or rabbits' feet. Some believe they are in possession of some type of magic tool. But God is not a vending machine that dispenses goods at the sound of a particular formula. To place one's trust in anything other than God is idolatry, and to buy something in the hope of making something else happen is simply witchcraft. The Bible refers to this as divination. These trinkets are distractions that move us away from placing our faith in the true source of power—Jesus Christ.

Selling trinkets is nothing new. In 1517, a Catholic priest named Martin Luther rejected the idea to sell indulgences to raise money to rebuild St. Peter's Basilica in Rome. People were told that they could buy their way out of sin by purchasing trinkets from the church, and this made Luther furious. He understood that this scheme made the people assume their sins were forgiven if they bought their way out. So he wrote a letter of ninety-five protest points challenging the church's authority on the subject, and he nailed the letter to the door of the church. Because he would not back down regarding this issue, he was ejected from the Catholic Church.

The church (Catholic) did not have a scriptural leg to stand on, but still they argued that they were the ruling body and could do pretty much anything they wanted. And the reason it was such an issue for the church was that selling indulgences was an important source of income, especially in lean times. Think about it: most of the church's problems, even in our day, stem from the issue of money.

Hirelings are all about money and always resurface from the mire to promote the new building fund, the pastor's appreciation day (even though it lasts a week, sometimes the entire month), or a new "vision" from God. Even during economic downturns and recessions they are skilled at twisting Scripture to cause people to feel guilty so they will give money. Second Peter says that "with eyes full of adultery, they never stop sinning; they seduce the unstable; they are experts in greed—an accursed brood! (2:14). Hirelings may say that our giving money actually "activates our faith." Such words are a huge red flag. Giving money is no guarantee that anyone has true faith. The Pharisees were big givers of money (Matt. 6:2–4), but Jesus declared they were a brood of vipers and were condemned to hell (Matt. 23:33).

When Simon the Sorcerer thought he could buy the gift of God with money, he was willing to give a donation to possess the abilities the apostles had. But Peter said he had no true faith at all and that his heart was not right before God (Acts 8:18–23). *I am convinced that if Simon were alive today, a lot of leaders would have taken his "seed faith" money, anointed him and given him an eldership position.* Nowhere in all of Scripture is it implied that someone has to pay to be forgiven, or pay for healing, or pay for a personal prophetic Word from the Lord. It grieves my heart to hear that some so-called prophets are teaching that money activates the prophetic gifting. Supposedly, this teaching is taken from the concept that one cannot stand before a prophet empty-handed (without a gift). *Beware: The gifts of the Spirit and money do not mix! If you are in a church service and begin to see spiritual gifts operating with the goal of raising money, run!* It does not matter how accurate these gifts may appear, they do not indicate a move of the Spirit of the Lord.

This is another example of stretching a verse of Scripture way out of context. The modus operandi of every hireling is clever Scripture-twisting. It is the art of pulling the text out of context to support their pretext. It is to corrupt the correct meaning of Scripture to supply a different meaning which supports the hireling's point of view or agenda (2 Cor. 4:2). Know this: Jesus of Nazareth was and is the greatest prophet who ever lived. Nowhere in the Word of God do we see Jesus demanding an offering for a prophetic word or healing. Make no mistake about it, this kind of teaching is perverted and far off the mark.

Everything a hireling does is for the sake of money. He is a mercenary—one who works only to receive pay. A hireling will not speak at a church if there is no money involved. He will not speak at your church or event unless he can "raise" his own offering after he has spoken. Many hirelings will not speak unless they can be guaranteed an offering of a certain size. In the final analysis, money is his underlying motivation, and he is not of God.

There is nothing new under the sun. Paul dealt with the same thing in the church of Corinth. In the Greek culture of Paul's time, the more popular you were as a speaker, the more money you could demand. Asking and getting big money for speaking meant you were a great speaker. But since Paul did not ask for any money, the people figured his preaching was not worth hearing (2 Cor. 11:5–9). This left room for the false teachers to alter the people's opinions about Paul. Eventually, the apostle was forced to defend his stance by saying that charging for the gospel was an abuse of authority (1 Cor. 9:18).

Flagrant hirelings have been known to schedule multiple engagements for the same time and cancel the lowest paying one at the last minute. They may also ask for large honorariums on top of a "love" offering. And because countless people flock to hear them speak, they tend to demand more and more money. The terrible thing is that the churches oblige them and pay more. Such corruption is so out of control that some churches take out bank loans to pay well-known speakers in hopes they will raise enough money when he comes to pay off the loan. I know of a very popular leader who was asked to speak at a particular church. After he spoke, he demanded such a huge offering that it left the church without any money to pay their utilities for the month. Let me repeat, the true laborer is worthy of his wages, but if money is his entire motivation for serving God, he is in big-time error and we should withdraw ourselves from him (1 Tim. 6:5).

True spiritual leaders are so humble and sensitive to the voice of God, he can use them anywhere, including churches with small congregations and limited financial resources. We all need to evaluate our church leadership and favorite preachers in light of these facts about hirelings.

## CHARACTER OF A HIRELING

A hireling is as predatory and destructive as a wolf. Essentially, they are wolves who, once in power, will not hesitate to prey on the flock. The hireling uses his spiritual authority for financial gain. Many churches have a well-deserved reputation for being all about money, and this has unfortunately turned away some who were searching for the real thing. The Enemy has risen up such leaders to hinder the search for the true message of Christ and keep sincere seekers from finding salvation. He also uses these leaders to alienate from the church those who have been turned off as a result of experiencing financial abuse.

A hireling is one who beats up his people emotionally and spiritually before they even realize what he has done. He makes them feel guilty if they fail to give and may go as far as to pronounce a curse upon them. Some are even bold enough to call one-on-one meetings regarding missed tithe payments. I have heard of several pastors who have invoiced their members past "tithe bills." Show me this type of behavior in the Word of God! They may even blame the lack of giving for other problems in the giver's life, as if God is punishing them. Such things are always wrong. As believers, we should give our best to God and should honor God sacrificially in our giving, but giving is not a cure-all pill. Ask King Saul (1 Sam. 15:10–23).

Hirelings give the impression that tithing is required to stay saved. They often promise that there will be blessings for giving even though the blessings are never manifested.

## "THE CHECK IS IN THE MAIL"

To show how some hirelings operate, a friend shared this:

"I have been in many services where the pastor (a hireling) would scan the audience to see how many people were there in order to come up with an amount for the members to give. On Sundays, there were the one-hundred dollar lines, where each individual in that line would receive a prophetic word. Sometimes four people would link up to give twenty-five dollars apiece to make a total of one-hundred dollars. In that case, the four people would receive one prophetic word. If one had nothing to give but a few dollars, that individual received only a general prayer. I remember one particular Sunday when I stood in the one-hundred dollar line and was told to check my mailbox in fourteen days because I would receive a check. Though I was not really expecting any checks, I did as I was told and checked my box on the fourteenth day. But the box was empty. After that mailbox experience I stopped getting in the money lines and I never believed the pastor again."

Hirelings are like dictators in that they oppress the people with a heavy weight of guilt which God never intended. And while sound doctrine teaches us to give, it says we are to give sacrificially and cheerfully out of the abundance of our grateful hearts. God does not want us giving out of obligation. Second Corinthians 9:7 says it so beautifully: "So let each one give as he purposes in his heart, *not grudgingly or of necessity,* for God loves a cheerful giver" (emphasis mine). Did you even know that passage was in the Bible? Or did your pastor conveniently neglect to mention it as he passed the offering plate for the third time? The answer to that question is the key to determining what kind of shepherd is leading you.

While a true shepherd will trust the sheep to be led by the Holy Spirit, a hireling will usurp the place of the Spirit because the trust factor with God is absent, and this is especially true on the subject of giving. And if a leader is a hireling, he will expose his true agenda by giving positions of honor to people who live in sin as long as they have something to offer (2 Chr. 13:9). These leaders also target and try to cultivate relationships with business owners and other entrepreneurs who are non-Christians but can benefit them financially in some way.

It is interesting to note that before we came to Christ we were easily able to spot a scam artist. Why is it, then, that after receiving salvation it is like we have decided not to use good judgment (otherwise known as brains) anymore? Remember, God has not taken away our ability to think and discern (Acts 17:10–11).

Hirelings often call us judgmental if we challenge them on a point that disagrees with Scripture. They constantly say things like, "Touch not God's anointed," and "Do his prophets no harm." This phrase, taken out of its context, is used so often by unscrupulous hirelings that we feel paralyzed when we hear it. It makes us terrified to question even the smallest problems, even when we know the preaching or teaching is wrong. And of course this is what the hireling wants. The actual meaning of this verse in Psalm 105 can be found in the first 11 verses. The psalmist was declaring how God keeps his covenant with the patriarchs and their decedents, and the next four verses were a reminder of his faithful care of them while they were traveling through foreign and hostile countries. Verse 15 proclaims that God didn't allow the evil kings to harm his people—the entire group—and he didn't allow his messengers to be physically harmed or killed by those kings. This verse has been repeated with wrong intent so long that evil leaders can practice their guile unashamedly, daring naïve and fearful followers to question their works.

And while it is true that we should not disrespect anyone, we do have a responsibility to ask questions if we don't understand, confront evil and refuse to support false shepherds who teach for dishonest gain and lead the unsuspecting into the trap of the Devil (Titus 1:10–11; 2 Tim. 2:24–26). If your leader is unapproachable and asking them questions is considered off limits, that's a good indicator that you need to seek the Lord for an exit plan.

Jesus said that he will not judge us, but the Word that we have heard *will* judge us in the end. He said, "As for the person who hears my words but does not keep them, I do not judge him. . . . There is a judge for the one who rejects me and does not accept my words; that very word which I spoke will condemn him at the last day" (John 12:47–48). It is this Word that demands a response. God does not have to do anything else to warn us because he has already given us the Word and the knowledge to make our own choices to either accept or reject it.

Many people will no doubt be shocked and horrified on judgment day to find out God does not know them and that their names are not written down in the Lamb's Book of Life. They will have failed to realize that the issue is not whether we think we know God but whether God knows us. Some of these people will claim even to have prophesied and cast out demons in God's name. They will ask, "Lord, Lord, did we not prophesy in your name, and in your name drive out demons and perform many miracles?" And then the Lord will respond, "I never knew you. Away from me, you evildoers!" (Matt. 7:21–23). So the million-dollar question is not, "Do you know God?" But, "Does God know you?"

Chapter 7

# CAUGHT UP IN TITLES

WE ALL ASSUME THAT THOSE WITH TITLES IN FRONT OF THEIR name are wise. Doctor, apostle, reverend and bishop all imply wisdom, whether or not the title holders actually are wise and actually know God. Some have acquired an education from a legitimate educational institution, and some are given honorary degrees based on their good works and impressive life experiences. Others "earned" their "degrees" via correspondence and online schools. Often these schools are nothing more than a post office box or an office suite with an impressive website that directs people where they can send money to buy their credentials. Many titles are un-awarded and unearned; some people simply claim for themselves a title. Many of these schools have a reputation of being a diploma mill for leaders. They award high-profile leaders with degrees in order to allure others to their schools. Having a degree from the same school as your favorite leader is a compelling draw for some people.

Hirelings use degrees and titles to build their credibility so that uninitiated people will believe they know whereof they speak. I am not saying that everyone who preaches or teaches must have a degree behind his name. But he must be well-versed in Scripture, have a mature walk with the Lord, and not be inclined to add or take away from the Word. And most of all, he must have a passion for seeing souls come to Christ.

If there is any question about where your leaders have been educated, take the time to investigate the certificates that line their office walls. Did they really graduate from accredited Christian seminaries and divinity schools with good reputations, or were they off-the-wall doctrinally? Did they have to write an academic dissertation to earn their doctorate? Go online and check out the foundational doctrines of those schools and see if they hold true to God's Word.

Did their course of study include hermeneutics or learning to interpret the Bible the way God intended? Did they study exegesis, which teaches students how to view Scripture in light of its context? At a legitimate school pastoral students also take classes in homiletics and expository Bible study. These courses teach students how to study and preach Scripture effectively in order to bring people to salvation and train them to study God's Word for themselves. A legitimate educational institution will not award a master's or doctorate degree unless the student shows proficiency at a high level in such courses. In the same way we would not allow an untrained person to build a skyscraper for us, or perform surgery on us, we dare not let an ill-equipped leader teach us about the things of God.

We can distinguish true shepherds by their fruit. Those interested only in titles and not in serious academic preparation may be charismatic speakers, but do they go beyond gobbledygook and double-talk? Perhaps they are eloquent, but the question is, what did they actually say? Was their well deep or shallow? Was anything important and memorable said, or was there nothing of substance worth remembering, as described in Jude 12?

It is deplorable that hirelings have overwhelmed the body of

Christ in the American church and have usurped the place of true shepherds for the purpose of defrauding the flock. As believers, we must learn to discern the difference between true shepherds, hirelings and dictators. We dare not take this subject lightly as it can cost many their souls.

This distinction between true and false shepherds was so important to Christ that he took time to warn people to beware of such teachers. He said, "Watch out for the teachers of the law. They like to walk around in flowing robes and be greeted in the marketplaces, and have the most important seats in the synagogues and the places of honor at banquets. They devour widows' houses and for a show make lengthy prayers. Such men will be punished most severely" (Mark 12:38–40).

Hirelings are quite predictable. Most are very charismatic and always make a pretense of liking you. They seek out those who are vulnerable and desperate for love and compassion. They also seek out those of status and substance. Either way, flattery is the method of choice—they are skilled at telling you what you want to hear in order to get something from you. But those who are under the influence of flattery will usually end up worse in the end than before. Proverbs 26:28 states, "A lying tongue hates those who are crushed by it, and a flattering mouth works ruin."

The interesting thing is that these hirelings quickly disappear when you have nothing of value to offer. Armed with this information, you can evaluate whether or not your pastor loves to associate only with the wealthy or if he shows no discrimination and loves the poor and rich alike. Is he like Jesus, showing no favoritism, as advised in James 2:1–9?

In order to devour someone like a wolf, a hireling must first isolate the person, shower him or her with attention, affirmation and affection, and then make that person believe no one else loves them or understands them like he does. Usually, his affection lasts only until the money runs out. When you have no more to offer the hireling, his attitude changes, and he goes on to greener pastures. And though you may have once been his favorite person, in the end he forgets and ignores you.

Warning: Wolves eat sheep. They take note of your possessions and see them as prizes that are up for grabs.

### How to Guard Against Becoming Prey

Much of the church is made up of single women or women whose husbands want nothing to do with God, which is why it is so common to see hirelings moving in. Wolves often prey on such women and take captive those who are emotional and gullible. "They are the kind who worm their way into homes and gain control over weak-willed women, who are loaded down with sins and are swayed by all kinds of evil desires" (2 Tim. 3:6). It is a known fact that once these wolves are allowed into someone's life that someone is devoured. The reason this works so well is that there are few men in these churches with the courage and ability to call such men to account.

There are some hirelings who, over time, become more intimidating and bolder. No longer subtle, they take up several offerings in a single service. And because the people have no discernment in spiritual matters, they are taken in, deceived to believe God will bless them because they submit. (*Whoever said that submission to God demands that we submit to a leader who is leading us into sin?*) Though we should respect our pastors as we would anyone else, no pastor is equal to God, and no pastor's word is infallible.

Most of those who rarely attend church can instantly identify excessive offerings as a scam. Why is it that some church members have no clue to this fraud and have swallowed the party line—hook, line and sinker? It should be obvious to any thinking individual that such leaders are not of God. They are nothing but con artists and thieves.

Jesus warned that wolves would show up and not in wolves' clothing. They will be dressed as shepherds who fleece the flock to fill their own pockets, often buying Bentleys, Benzes, jets, and traveling with teams of body guards. Many televangelists clearly fit the category of hirelings, and their deplorable prosperity message (God wants everyone to be successful and rich) is all the more enticing to those who are desperate due to poor economic situations and to loss of jobs and retirement savings, or simply just greed. It takes a very strong sense of spiritual discernment not to be sucked in by these empty promises, especially when the televangelists teach that God will come through in response to sacrificial giving. The truth is, God says, he will not be mocked. Whatever these men (and some women) sow, they will reap in eternity (Gal. 6:7–8). Those who prey upon the poor, widows and the needy will heap to themselves greater judgment than anyone else because they did it knowingly and without apology (Prov. 22:22–23). In the end, God will plunder those who plunder his children, for they are without excuse.

Chapter 8

# STUDY TO SHOW THYSELF APPROVED

BECAUSE GOD HAS GIVEN US HIS WORD, THE HOLY SPIRIT, AND the ability to discern, there is absolutely no excuse for ignorance. We are each to study the Bible for ourselves and get into the secret place where we grasp God's intent behind that Word. If we equip ourselves, we will not be deceived when false teachers twist the truth to suit their own designs.

The sad truth is that anyone can make the Bible say anything they want it to say. Think back to the tragic story of Jim Jones, who started out as a Pentecostal preacher. Because he had a charismatic personality he could easily move the emotions of his people. Over time he even convinced the unsuspecting to sell what they owned to follow him to an isolated, distant land. He taught from the Bible, but his unorthodox approach to Bible teaching had a tragic twist that ended up costing hundreds their lives. Most cults are born like this, with persons of charismatic persuasion perverting the true meaning of Scripture and corrupting naïve and unsuspecting Christians. Only if God's people are equipped with scriptural wisdom and discernment can they defend themselves against such overwhelming charlatanism (Phil. 1:9–11).

It feels foreign to the average churchgoer to worry about what the church does with his or her money. For so long it has been wrongly assumed that we can simply attend church, give our time and money, and go home feeling better than when we arrived. But this is not what God intended. God wants us to be sure our leaders are fiscally responsible, accountable and trustworthy individuals of integrity who take pains to do what is right (2 Cor. 8:16–24).

Contrary to popular opinion, it is not hard to grow a large, "successful" church—as long as anything goes. It will explode in growth if the preacher is appealing and eloquent, people-pleasing, and if he preaches on topics that are popular and not very demanding from a spiritual point of view. Too many in the church today are fans of men but not so much disciples of Christ. In America, we are a celebrity-driven culture, and that mindset has made its way into the church. It's a disheartening thing to say, but we are more divided over personalities than we are over destructive doctrines. We display greater allegiance to men than we show to Christ. It's shocking! Such leaders are the sort of preachers mentioned in Jude 4, who slip into the church to do as much damage as they can: "They are godless men, who change the grace of our God into a license for immorality and deny Jesus Christ our only Sovereign and Lord." Then to top off the cake, the misleading shepherd will comfort the people in their sins by saying, "God's grace will cover you." This is a calamity of unequalled proportions because here's a sad truth: men and women will die in their sins, never realizing they are unprepared to meet God.

## People-Pleasing Leaders

Consider this: Jesus, who is one with God, our Creator, once fed over five thousand souls with just two fish and five bread loaves. But after Jesus died, there were only 120 who awaited the coming of the Holy Spirit in the Upper Room. The Lord Jesus, who had everything at his fingertips, refused to change his message to suit the masses. How dare we do otherwise?

The most popular churches today are those calling themselves *purpose-driven*. These churches are *seeker-friendly* or *seeker-sensitive*, meaning that they gear the services to suit the listeners. They are often referred to as "drive-thru churches" because they get people in and out quickly, and everything is done according to a set schedule. For example, worship lasts fifteen minutes, another fifteen is set aside for the collection of tithes and offerings, then the pastor preaches for twenty-five minutes, and afterward the church is dismissed. Some pastors and executive staff even go so far as to survey their people and the community, asking, "What would you like to see in church?" Then they customize the services to meet the wants and desires of the people. As a result, many of these churches have reduced the offense of the Cross and eliminated the need for a Savior and Lord. They don't preach on sin; indeed, they do not even mention the word *sin*, but instead use words like "dysfunction," "mishaps," "mistakes" and "issues." Altar calls, as you can imagine, are a thing of the past.

A huge draw to these types of churches is the offer of free lattes and fresh donuts in the foyer, where newcomers can feel welcomed. These churches even take special care to train greeters to make guests feel at home. Some churches offer plays and skits instead of preaching the unvarnished Word of God. Too many purpose-driven church leaders customize churches according to the wishes of individuals who really do not want God. Some people do not want to be convicted of their sin, and they think they have no need for repentance. In the end, how many visitors are sent home with their hearts in the same condition as when they walked in?

In a recent poll, over seventy percent of the people in the United States claimed to be Christians, but of those, over fifty percent believe there is more than one way to heaven. Talk-show hostess Oprah Winfrey teaches that there is more than one way to heaven. Even with this belief, she calls one of the most popular church leaders in our time her pastor; that's disturbing. She should know (or be told) that Scripture says otherwise, and in no uncertain terms. In John 14:6, Jesus said, "I am the way, the truth and the life. No man comes to the Father but by me." What sort of preaching philosophy has taken hold of the church in America when the churches fail to proclaim that Jesus is not a way, but is the only way to heaven? It is the seeker-sensitive philosophy.

God is not a problem to these churches. Because he is unseen, his character can easily be distorted. It is the concept of sin and Jesus' sacrificial death on a cross that is a stumbling block to those who refuse to repent. Muslims, Mormons, gays, the ACLU, Christian Science, the Unity Church, the metaphysical cults and all manner of others have no problem with an obscure God. But they all deny that Jesus came in the flesh as the one and only Savior of humankind. This fact is a problem because it requires a response—and the only correct response is repentance.

## SAFEGUARD YOURSELVES BY STAYING WITHIN THE BOUNDARIES

The aging apostle John warns his beloved children in the faith about entertaining heresy rather than truth:

"I say this because many deceivers have gone out into the world. They deny that Jesus Christ came in a real body. Such a person is a deceiver and an antichrist. Watch out that you do not lose what we have worked so hard to achieve. Be diligent so that you receive your full reward. Anyone who wanders away from this teaching has no relationship with God. But anyone who remains in the teaching of Christ has a relationship with both the Father and the Son. If anyone comes to your meeting and does not teach the truth about Christ, don't invite that person into your home or give any kind of encouragement. Anyone who encourages such people becomes a partner in their evil work" (2 John 7–11).

Even associating with those who teach less than the full gospel of Christ signifies approval on our part, and that will, in no uncertain terms, bring judgment.

Consider the words, *"wander beyond."* The idea of wandering beyond something stems from the word *trespass,* meaning to cross over a set boundary, or to move into something that's off-limits. John warns us to be on guard lest we cross over the boundary and no longer abide in Jesus. In other words, we dare not be fooled into believing we can live our lives without limits. To do so is transgression, crossing the line.

Because God loves us and knows us intimately, he set boundaries at Creation that would protect us and help us flourish. Scripture never tells us to do whatever we please. It is only the Devil and his ministers who invite us to do and think as we please, so that we miss the mark and remain forever lost to God's plan (Matt. 4:4–10).

It is so easy to fall for Satan's line because he says exactly what we want to hear. It is a sad irony that getting what we want can, in the end, kill us. God measures our love by how much we are willing to obey him and stay within his boundaries. In essence, God, through the apostle John, warns us not to entertain anyone offering us freedom beyond God's pre-set limits. For these men—even if they are leaders of megachurches—are the "enemies of the Cross of Christ" (Phil. 3:18).

The apostle James warns, "Anyone who encourages such people becomes a partner in their evil work" (2 John 11). When the Bible says we are not to receive or invite such men into our house, it means we are not to financially support them or their ministries in any way. And it means we are not to invite them into our worship services or give them a platform on which to teach heresy. To financially support and to give advertisement to such men is committing accessory to the crime. Aiding someone is just as bad as the one who is performing it; and God says that person has become a partner with what is evil. Do we want the Lord on Judgment Day to tell us to depart because of our financial support and our social media sharing of false leaders? Knowing such warning should make us alert to our actions of indirectly strengthening the hands of evil doers. We are to walk away and have nothing to do with them lest we share their judgment.

Chapter 9

# A LACK OF DISCERNMENT

THERE HAVE ALWAYS BEEN THOSE WHO DECEIVE THE unsuspecting into supporting their devious cause, but there is nothing worse than using God's precious provision to support a traitorous teacher. Many people in the church are guilty of doing exactly this. They say or think that if they give their money God will make them healthy and wealthy. They feel secure with the idea that whatever the pastor does with the money is between him and God. But God takes very seriously how we spend our resources. In the same way that he says not to associate with delusory teachers in any way, he holds us accountable for what he gives us and tells us not to bless those who curse him. This includes self-appointed teachers. And while they may not come right out and curse God openly (because that would be too obvious), in their hearts false teachers preach another gospel, and thereby curse God. Remember, Scripture says that those who are not with Jesus are against him (Matt. 12:30). Scripture cannot be any more straightforward than that. We will all be judged along with the false prophet if we refuse to walk away from diabolical teaching (Jer. 14:14–16).

The reason wolves are able to operate so openly in today's

church is because undiscerning sheep support them financially. If they didn't, devious teachers would have folded their tents and moved on long ago. And if God takes this situation so seriously, we need to do likewise, knowing we will invite the wrath of the Lord if we help the wicked (2 Chr. 19:2).

In exactly the same way, we have raised up an entire generation of immature believers, and we have even trained some to become pastors who speak *Christianese* with the best of us. But they do so with an ulterior motive. They use Scripture out of context to proof-text their personal prejudices and pet theologies—all to defraud and deceive the flock. Many are very charming and persuasive in temperament, and they could probably sell a boat to someone living in the desert. While they may say the right words, they spin them to mean something other than what God intended.

If a shepherd refuses to talk about sin and the need to repent and be holy, he is plainly preaching another gospel. If he does not mention spiritual maturity, righteousness and having a passion for Christ, he is preaching another gospel. If he does not encourage his congregation to love thy neighbor and win souls, he is preaching another gospel. If he will not talk about denying oneself, picking up the cross and following Christ in obedience, he is preaching another gospel. If he does not teach about the lordship of Christ, he is preaching another gospel.

It has been said that false knowledge is more dangerous than true ignorance. I believe this is accurate because true ignorance is a lack of understanding; one just does not know. But false knowledge *thinks* it knows, even when the knowledge is wrong. Those who quote the Bible out of context to prove a point are risking eternal judgment because they have false knowledge and have poisoned the true gospel of Jesus Christ and fed it to their people.

In our day there are many things believed to be of God that

previously would have been called blasphemy or heresy. Many things we think are anointed with the Holy Spirit would, in the past, have been seen as demonic or of the flesh. This is because our Christian ancestors could discern spirits in ways many of us simply cannot. When we are not knowledgeable regarding the context of a certain Scripture, we may erroneously conclude that if something works or seems supernatural, it has to be of God, especially if the preacher said it. Such thinking sets us up for deceptions by false signs and wonders (2 Thess. 2:9). In fact, one of the Enemy's most effective weapons is the use of partial truth mixed with lies. He will take what is familiar and taint it with error—and then sell us a bill of goods that sounds right but is not of God. There are even times when only people with heightened discernment will have a check in their spirits, realizing that what they saw or heard was not of God. One biblical example of this was Paul, who discerned that the slave girl who boldly predicted the future was demonic (Acts 16:16–18). In today's church, because of the accuracy of her gift, we would have called her a prophetess and supported her prophetic conferences.

## COMFORTABLE IN SIN

Unbiblical manifestations were in evidence when a friend visited a church:

> "My family attended a spirit-filled church where the Wednesday night service was all about youth. Because our children were in their early teens, they wanted to try it. I accompanied them the first night and stood on the sidelines to watch. What I saw frightened me. The pastor's wife was in charge, and they had praise and worship. Although signs and wonders were in evidence, it wasn't the spirit of God operating in that group. At first I couldn't believe my eyes. When I asked

the Lord what it was, he revealed that it was the spirit of entertainment, not the spirit of Christ. Later I overheard the conversation of two teen girls, and the conversation went something like, "So what do you think?" "Not bad. Good place to pick up guys and drugs. Think she knows we cast spells when we're not here?" It occurred to me that even in church these kids were not uncomfortable in their sin. My children did not return to that church's Wednesday night youth service."

Scripture says that in the last days the Enemy will use signs, wonders, miracles and healings that are anything but anointed by God. Jesus said, "False Christs and false prophets will appear and perform great signs and miracles to deceive even the elect" (Matt. 24:24). And if that is so, they are of the Devil. And those without discernment will be taken in and deceived, believing it is all of God. In reality, the Devil is just as capable of using the supernatural as God is. And using the supernatural is how many people are taken in. It is so very vital we become discerning and really know God and his Word. Right now, God is drawing his church back to the basics, back to the parameters of his revealed Word. He is eager to sharpen our discernment and equip us for our protection. People often quote verses they have memorized, but they still lack spiritual maturity and have not been trained to rightly divide the Word of Truth. Many have repeated salvation prayers, but they have never submitted to the lordship of Christ. They continue living in disobedience and rebellion and refuse to surrender to God even when the Holy Spirit convicts them. Sometimes these people are put in leadership positions because they have natural gifts, but they quickly become a liability to the body if they do not live according to righteousness.

James, the brother of Jesus, says "My brethren, let not many of you become teachers, knowing that we shall receive a stricter judgment" (3:1). This means that if leaders understood the terrible accountability that accompanies preaching and teaching, they would not be so quick to assume leadership duties. God holds leaders more accountable because they are in places of influence.

Christians often fail to grasp the seriousness of this subject. They personally do not know the Lord well enough to understand what is of God and what is not. Just because a person has memorized Scripture does not mean he or she is applying or teaching it according to God's intent.

In the same way, just because someone carries himself like a spiritual leader does not mean he has a true heart for God. He may have found that by saying the right words he can weasel his way into others' good graces and get what he wants—status, power or wealth. Yet such an attitude sets him up for eternal damnation. This is why it is so essential to compare what we see and hear with God's Word. We do this with the help of the Holy Spirit and the spirit of discernment.

Those who use the pulpit to express their personal opinions instead of preaching God's Word are out of order. The church must beware if all it hears is, "I think . . .," "I feel . . .," or "It is my opinion that . . . ." We must allow the Bible to speak for itself and not try speaking for it. Paul told Timothy to preach the Word. This means a leader should never use the pulpit to persuade people of his perspective; rather, he should teach exactly what the Bible says.

### DRIVEN BY EMOTIONS

Many churches are driven by emotion rather than substance. People are far too easily moved by emotion, and usually attribute their behavior to the power of the Holy Spirit moving in the service. That is not necessarily true at all. Many feel they have not had church unless they shout, shake or fall to the floor. But this is merely a show of emotion and no evidence of substance. The true test of whether the Holy Spirit has moved is real and lasting heart transformation.

Many often cannot distinguish the difference. Some people are easily bored with the simple, direct teaching of the Word. They want excitement. Many in this generation have been fed a steady diet of fast-moving video games, social media posting and constant texting. It is no wonder that sitting still and listening seems dull to them. Let's face it, excitement sells! The gospel? Not so much. If churchgoers have no intention of changing but only want hype and visual stimulation, they will not sit long under sound teaching. And as hard as it is to believe, there are actually places that do nothing but teach pastors how to "whoop" and holler to hype up the emotions of the crowd. This may or may not be done to simulate a real move of God, but it does satisfy the people's need for emotion.

Anytime someone with scriptural knowledge begins to grow cold and walk away from God's Word, there is a good possibility that person will become self-righteous and feel the rules no longer apply. To outsiders they look holy because they are book-smart regarding God's Word, but that does not mean they live it. When this happens to pastors they become a danger not only to themselves but to others, going from bad to worse, deceiving and being deceived (2 Tim. 3:13). It has been said that the hardest people to convince are those who believe they already know the answers.

For a pastor who was at one time walking the narrow way and preaching the true Word of God, it's also easy to begin to take credit for the blessing of God when numbers start to increase. When the ministry flourishes and people line up at the door bringing their cash with them, it does not take much persuasion to convince such leaders that they have made it. They like being singled out. They love being seen. This is exactly how

Scripture describes the Pharisees of Jesus' day. Jesus told them, "You are the ones who justify yourselves in the eyes of men, but God knows your hearts. What is highly valued among men is detestable in God's sight" (Luke 16:14–15).

In our day they may not call themselves Pharisees, but they do exactly the same things. For example, during church services, they often sit in their "study" waiting to make their grand entrance. Then, as the choir begins singing "How Great Thou Art," they make their way down to the pulpit, security guards preceding them, with "armor-bearers," a title that has no meaning in the New Testament church but is simply a position that controlling leaders can use to dominate the faith and will of others. People have suffered great embarrassment and shame through this unbiblical role in today's church. Don't get me wrong, having a heart to serve in the church is a great gift, but a majority of what's displayed through armor-bearing is anything but true service to God; it has become a glorified slave position for the unqualified leader. Those who are serving are made to think they are saved and God is pleased with them because they are serving the individual. But neglecting your own family to run errands and babysit for leaders, free of charge, is a great indicator that many are not serving Christ, rather man. Does this sound familiar? How many pastors who stage this sort of thing have left the narrow way and gone in another direction entirely? How many preach the Word to their people while knowingly disobeying it in their own lives? How many deny the true Word and water down the message so that it lacks the power to convict? Beware of any leader who belittles and scorn those who serve.

Many televangelists who are currently quite popular and highly visible fit this description. They may have begun preaching the true Word, but somewhere along the way they gave in to compromise, started tickling ears, and kept from offending wealthy donors to cultivate popularity. Fans generally see them as approved by God merely because of their great visibility and growing number of followers. They fail to realize that worldly success and increasing numbers alone have nothing to do with actual godliness.

The time has come when God is shaking everything, starting with the household of faith. He wants to separate what is truth from a lie. He does this to bring us back to his original intent, to the Word, where we must start fresh, pressing in to the secret place, and worshiping in spirit and in truth.

Regardless of how much we like or respect a teacher, we must inspect his fruit to see if it stands or falls. Regardless of the numbers that follow him, if his teaching is out of line or does not measure up with Scripture, it is not of God (Rom. 16:17–18). If this describes your place of worship, it is time to leave.

Chapter 10

# FREEDOM FROM FALSE LEADERS

WHEN WE REMAIN UNDER THE TEACHING OF UNFAITHFUL leaders, we actually reinforce their wayward behavior. They are most likely to take our continuous support as approval and become even bolder, as they move in the flesh rather than in the Spirit of God.

Eventually, these leaders come to a point where they assume they can teach anything, whether it is right or wrong, and the people won't object. Charles Spurgeon made a powerful prophetic statement over a century ago that speaks to our generation. He said, "Everywhere there is apathy. Nobody cares whether that which is preached is true or false, a sermon is a sermon whatever the subject; only, the shorter it is the better." How many attending churches in America today have the same feeling? And when church-goers have this spiritless attitude, dangerous leaders become very comfortable asking their people for unreasonable things God has never required, including huge sums of wealth, real estate or other material goods. They are able to get away with such things because of the apathy of most Christians who not only allow it but have come to expect it.

Why is this erroneous practice so common and so blatant?

Because we have not studied to show ourselves approved unto God, rightly dividing the Word of Truth (2 Tim. 2:15) from falsehoods. We have not confronted such behavior with Scripture and called a spade a spade. Instead of digging into Scripture to know God, we have accepted the words of charlatans, wolves in sheep's clothing, and we have gone along with behaviors that would have never been allowed if the body of Christ had called them on it (2 Cor. 11:13–20). We do not discern the truth because we do not evaluate teaching in light of Scripture.

Those who have come out of counterfeit teaching often testify that they were blinded by charisma, and until the Holy Spirit revealed the truth they absolutely could not see through the deception. This is much like being in love and overlooking warning signs of abuse in your beloved. Even if a man is unfaithful, and the warning signs are there, some women disregard them, denying reality, thinking they are either overreacting or seeing things. And though friends may warn them, they refuse to face the truth until it is far too late and they are in over their heads and cannot escape. At that point the abused get upset with themselves and others because they have been deceived, humiliated, scarred and perhaps even impoverished by a fraud.

People endure many painful things when they believe God is trying to teach them something. But they should know that God will never risk their souls to hell for the sake of a lesson. And though we may at first be blind to problems in a leader, once we have seen the light we must avail ourselves of the first chance to escape.

In truth, many times we are the ones refusing to let go. We have been sucked in, enamored and have fallen in love with an evil system. Sometimes we try to hold on even when we know it is not working. Often God has already opened doors of escape, and yet we keep going back like a moth to a destructive flame.

We may already have a witness in our spirits, but still things must really get worse before we are fed up and realize we have no other choice but to leave. At that point, it is time to shake the dust off our shoes and move on.

Some of us repeatedly set ourselves up for the same kind of behaviors that allow false leaders to take control, even knowing it did not work before. In some ways it is like an addiction we must keep feeding. How many times do we have to be promised that if we sow a seed we will see millions of dollars in ninety days? How many more messages do you need to hear about you coming out of debt if you give this particular amount of money? How many times will you believe if you sow a seed God is going to save your marriage or your loved ones? It is interesting that the very people who told you to sow a seed for your marriage often have ended up in divorce. How many times will we hear and believe that "a sinner's wealth is stored up for the righteous," as Proverbs 13:22 says?

*While on this subject, I must note that those who teach about a transfer of the world's wealth never received their wealth from the world. They received it from us, the church.* These leaders will try to convince the masses that they did not become wealthy from the church but yet received their wealth from investments or businesses. This is deceitful and dishonest speech. If it was not for the church money they would not have a business. Do we really believe God will give us a one-hundred-times-blessing for every dollar we sow? Let us not forget what the Bible says about false teachers and their destruction: "In their greed they will make up clever lies to get a hold of your money. But God condemned them long ago, and their destruction is on the way" (2 Pet. 2:3 NLT). What happened to common sense? What happened to "If it sounds too good to be true it probably is?"

Just because someone calls himself God's man—or woman —does not mean that person is not in it for the money. How many times do we have to be fleeced before we stop and ask ourselves, "Where does it say that in the context of Scripture?" In the final analysis, if the Scripture does not say it, it is wrong. If it had been of God in the first place, that million-dollar blessing would have manifested exactly on time.

The reason a questionable leader gives a ninety-day deadline is because that gives him an out, usually enough time for the beguiled to forget his prophetic lie. Scandalous prophets are notorious for victim-blaming when prophecies go unfulfilled. They claim the deceived misunderstood, or that they never said it to begin with, or that the misled did not have the requisite amount of faith. But whatever the reason, it is never the fault of the leader. I am sure this rings bells for many readers.

When these things happen we often want to blame God, and yet if we are honest, we must take responsibility for not staying true to the Word. These situations with false prophets have nothing to do with God. The real issue is what is going on in our own lives to make us fall for get-rich-quick schemes? Why are we so driven by greed? If we would choose instead to love and trust God, demanding nothing in return, no one would ever be able to defraud us.

That brings up the subject of contentment. It is the internal satisfaction and disposition of peace in the mind that is free from any external circumstance. Contentment is a product of being submitted to the will of God and not governing one's life based on what one does or does not have. It is probably true that our culture struggles more than any other when it comes to being content with less than the best. Compared to most others in the world, we (Americans) do have the best. Some may say, "So why not always expect the best to make us content?" Yet where in Scripture are we ever promised these things? One sin that is not preached much in our churches is covetousness (Luke 12:13–34). Greed and pursuing things that are off-limits by God have been redefined by terms such as "goals" and "ambition." The Holy Spirit will never lead anyone to teach something that promotes idolatry—it is man's attempt to use God, only to serve man's desires, purposes and wishes. Jesus never said we would all be rich. In fact, he often taught that money could be a stumbling block, a temptation and a snare (1 Tim. 6:1–11). He said, "No servant can serve two masters; for he will hate the one and love the other, or he will be devoted to the one and despise the other. You cannot serve both God and mammon" (Luke 16:13). We will never be content unless we love God first and have a heart to use what we already have to promote the gospel of Christ. If we have that kind of heart, we cannot be fleeced and defrauded. If we have hidden God's Word in our hearts and have pressed in to that secret place, we will know his plans for us— and not some delusional prophet's plans for us.

Many in our day are peddling the Word of God for profit and making it say things God never intended (see 2 Cor. 2:17 and 4:2), especially when it comes to giving and what is called a "first fruits offering." This is a repulsive scam that sounds so selfless but actually bilks the naïve every time. According to the first letter to the Corinthians and in the book of Acts, our first fruits offering is not money but Jesus, who was the first to rise from the dead, as the apostle Paul explains in 1 Cor. 15:20 and Acts 26:23. In the Old Testament, the first fruits offering was given during the Passover to consecrate future harvests. All offerings were a type and shadow of Christ. When Jesus was offered up it was during Passover, which consecrated and pointed to a coming harvest of souls into the kingdom of God. But today, the dishonest teachers run the scam by saying that if we give our best and largest gift first (some teach this means giving up your first paycheck at the beginning of the year), we then will have more than enough (an abundance) for the rest of the year. They are so persuasive in this claim that many leave their people struggling to pay their bills while the leader enjoys the fruits of their labors, often in the lap of luxury, growing "fat and sleek" (Jer. 5:26–28). I often wonder how they can look themselves in the mirror knowing they are victimizing their friends and brothers and sisters in Christ. But in their warped minds, they think they deserve it, though they did no legitimate work to earn it. As Solomon has said, "Food gained by fraud tastes sweet, but one ends up with a mouth full of gravel" (Prov. 20:17 NLT). And "Ill-gotten treasures are of no value, but righteousness delivers from death" (Prov. 10:2 NLT).

It must break God's heart to see these things happen so openly and so often in his church, because they are so far from his intent. Scripture says that such teachers will be punished more severely for taking advantage of the poor, widows and the unwary (Luke 20:45–47).

Unscrupulous teachers conveniently tell their people that their lack of prosperity is due to a lack of faith. Blame-shifting is a huge red flag that should make us sit up and pay attention. In reality, the reason such prophecies do not come to pass is because God never spoke them in the first place. After all, "Who can speak and have it happen if the Lord has not decreed it?" (Lam. 3:37 NLT). Be warned, God will never stand behind a promise he did not make. And while he may still bring us out of such teaching, it is wise to consider the loss of money, and sometimes possessions, as a very expensive and unforgettable lesson.

God is weary of people misusing his name for ill-gotten gain. It angers him to see people falling for a scam. When the disciples followed Jesus, he began warning them about holiness and hypocrisy and shedding light on the ulterior motives of false teachers (Luke 12:1–3). Many, especially those drawn in by signs, wonders and miracles, turned away, believing it was too hard to follow Christ. That was because they wanted an easy salvation that required no change of heart or behavior.

If the Spirit of God is not in operation in a church setting, the spirit of the Antichrist (Satan) is. And if we are not grounded in the Word we may be attracted to the counterfeit spirit at work there. These seducing spirits can easily fool the gullible who are less than discerning. In fact, because such an atmosphere is so non-confrontational, we can become comfortable in this kind of church and talk about it to others, actually drawing them in. In this way, the Enemy will use us to seduce others to their ultimate damnation, which as a result will bring harm to the body of Christ. Author and theologian John Warwick Montgomery once said, "The church can be a place of accelerated salvation; but it can also be a place of accelerated damnation." We dare not gamble with the souls of those God loves, for He will also hold us accountable for leading the innocent astray (Mark 9:42).

Preaching about seducing and the danger of evil spirits that deceive the ignorant and the innocent are not the sort of messages we hear much of anymore. But it happens all the time and this should make us very cautious about the arrogant and prideful teachers we sit under. Jesus' words are recorded in Matthew 18:3–6:

> "Assuredly, I say to you, unless you are converted and become as little children, you will by no means enter the kingdom of heaven. Therefore whoever humbles himself as this little child is the greatest in the kingdom of heaven. But whoever causes one of these little ones who believe in Me to sin, it would be better for him if a millstone were hung around his neck, and he were drowned in the depth of the sea."

We must never forget that when we sit under misleading teachers our children are also being led astray. Do we want to be held responsible for allowing such things? If we stay in a church that is in error, God will judge us for not protecting our children. Think about it. Most of us would do anything to protect our children, so will we leave for their benefit if not for our own?

## BEWARE OF THOSE WHO WILL LAY A BURDEN ON YOU THAT GOD DOES NOT

An often misunderstood Scripture is Matthew 11:28:

"Come unto Me, all you who labor and are heavy laden and I will give you rest. Take My yoke upon you and learn from Me, for I am gentle and lowly in heart, and you will find rest for your souls. For My yoke is easy and My burden is light."

It is misunderstood when teachers apply it to those who are physically fatigued. That, however, is not what Jesus meant. Rather, he was speaking about those who were heavily laden under the rule of the Pharisees, who had made it their job to devise an ever-increasing web of laws no human being could possibly follow. In fact, scribes, whose original function was merely to record Scripture passages word for word for future generations, actually began to misinterpret and add and subtract to what God had said. Over the years, this practice increased to the point where new scribes simply expounded on the opinions of other scribes who had gone before. The system was a flagrant departure from what God originally intended and, thereby, became an empty and meaningless exercise that never drew people to God. In fact, it alienated them.

In Jesus' day, the ceremonial traditions were very intricate and required participants to go to great lengths to join the synagogues. They had to pay various assessment fees, give funds for this and that, attend superfluous functions and so on; it was more like a social club steeped in mystery and tradition than a place of worship. Does this sound like the church you attend? In time, many simply gave up trying to get to God because it had become so laborious, complex and expensive. Who could blame them?

When Jesus came on the scene he shamed those who had made the way to God so complicated. He rebuked them for raking in riches at the expense of the poor and needy, for flaunting their power and for exempting themselves from rules. When Jesus cleansed the temple, recorded in John 2:13–16, he was acting out publicly against such traditions. He had no place for corrupt religious rulers and did not care if they were offended (Matt. 15:10–14), being that they pushed away those whom God loved, instead of welcoming them in.

Note what Jesus says in Mark 12:38–40:

"Beware of these teachers of religious law! For they love to parade in flowing robes and to have everyone bow to them as they walk in the marketplaces. And how they love seats of honor in the synagogues and at banquets. But they shamelessly cheat widows out of their property, and then, to cover up the kind of people they really are, they make long prayers in public. Because of this, their punishment will be greater" (NLT).

## TRUTH REQUIRES A RESPONSE

In Matthew chapter eleven, Jesus was addressing those who had been caught up in false religious systems. He let them know that if they were willing to unlearn what they had been taught, they could learn the simple gospel from him and find real rest for their souls. The only other option was to remain under the old system, where nothing would ever change and teachers would never admit they were wrong. During those years, the Law was distorted and often sounded so harsh that its original meaning was lost, and what was intended to draw the people to God actually drove them away. How many of us are attracted by rejection?

In order for the people to change their mindset they had to hear the truth about God. This is why Scripture says, "Faith comes by hearing, and hearing by the Word of God" (Rom. 10:17). Apart from a new revelation of who God is, as well as an impartation from the Holy Spirit, it is impossible for people to grasp the concept of salvation and their need of it.

Scripture says that the gospel is foolishness to the natural mind. It simply cannot be grasped apart from a spiritual awakening (1 Cor. 2:12–14). No matter how hard a person tries, no matter how sincere a person is, if one functions according to false teaching he or she cannot grasp the truth of the gospel. And those who swallow such false teaching as truth are in danger of hell.

Hosea 4:1–2 says, "Hear the word of the Lord, you children of Israel. For the Lord brings a charge against the inhabitants of the land: There is no truth or mercy, or knowledge of God in the land. By swearing and stealing and committing adultery they all break restraint, with bloodshed upon bloodshed . . . ."

The prophet says here in no uncertain terms that there is no knowledge of God in the land. Once again, the word *knowledge* does not refer to mere information. He is saying there was no progressive revelation of who God was. Hosea was asking how anyone can claim to know God while failing to live according to the whole counsel of the Word of God. These were teachers who chose to selectively teach things that would serve their own purposes while ignoring those things that did not. And though the people supposedly knew the true God, they had been sitting under false teaching and had learned nothing that would actually change their hearts or draw them into the presence of the living God.

Whenever we live inside the parameters of God's Word, there should be corresponding conduct in not only rightly dividing but rightly applying the Word of God. The new birth renders us dead to sin and alive to God, leaving no more room for the old self to function. There is no way a true believer can say he's living for Christ while practicing things that God says are sinful (1 John 1:5–6). We should be progressively growing not just in knowledge but in obedience to God. Hosea 4:6 records God's warning: "My people are destroyed for lack of knowledge. Because you have rejected knowledge I also will reject you from being priest for Me; because you have forgotten the law of your God, I also will forget your children." God was not saying they would die for lack of information. Instead, he was speaking to the priests who were failing to teach the people the truth of God's Word. And as a result, God's people were not being transformed by the renewing of their minds. Hence, the nation was suffering, falling into deception and chaos. He told the people that the more the priests' personal power increased, the more they sinned (v. 7). The more material things they collected, the more they sinned. It is dangerous to want more and not know God. In fact, greed is a glaring symptom of a civilization that has strayed far from God. No longer content with mere provision, greed begins to demand the best and the most of everything, until people wander from the faith and, as Paul cautioned Timothy, "pierced themselves with many griefs." (1 Tim. 6:6–10)

Many leaders in our day set their people up to fail. Like the Pharisees in Jesus' day, they erect an impossible standard and then they say, "Just do it." When the people fail, dishonest shepherds blame them and say their hearts are not right. They tell them that they failed to submit to God. The truth is, however, that it is the leaders themselves who have not submitted to God. The leaders are forcing the people to do what they themselves refuse to do (Luke 11:46). Following their example only leaves the people in despair and hopelessness, believing God is either a liar or impotent.

In Acts 20:28–31, Paul addresses the church. He likens a hireling to a wolf that does not spare the sheep but will do whatever it takes to get what it wants:

> "So guard yourselves and God's people. Feed and shepherd God's flock—his church, purchased with his own blood—over which the Holy Spirit has appointed you as leaders. I know that false teachers, like vicious wolves, will come in among you after I leave, not sparing the flock. Even some men from your own group will rise up and distort the truth in order to draw a following. Watch out! Remember the three years I was with you—my constant watch and care over you night and day, and my many tears for you" (NLT).

Wolves are never satisfied—they always want more. Paul is warning that once he leaves, evil teachers will move in and not spare the church. Then he addresses the leaders, cautioning them that if they are not careful they will begin straying from the truth of God and exalting themselves for personal gain. The motivation has never changed: fame, power, control and money. All of these come with large numbers of supporters when they tell people what they want to hear, rather than preaching the true Word of God. Such leaders become pragmatic, doing what is most beneficial to them rather than holding fast with God's original intent. They teach that if you feel like it is God, then it is God. Their modus operandi is to encourage the flock to do things according to how one feels rather than according to truth.

Pragmatism is counterproductive in God's kingdom. It fails to take into account that while God is love, he is also jealous and demands holiness. Make no mistake, in God's kingdom there are definite absolutes and definite standards we must uphold. Once we have a true revelation of who God is and are led by his Holy Spirit, we will not be fooled by every new wind of doctrine that blows past saying anything goes (Eph. 4:14).

When we get into the Bible and into God's presence, getting to know him intimately, we will be transformed by spending time with him and rightly dividing the Word of Truth. This is when we become truly dead to sin and alive to Christ. And we will love our brothers and sister more than ourselves, wanting their best rather than feeling critical, envious or intolerant. We will constantly examine our own hearts to see whether we have hidden sin, apathy regarding spiritual things, unforgiveness and bitterness, or other attitudes that are displeasing to God. In the end, what breaks God's heart should break our hearts. And if our leaders are not teaching us that model, they are not teaching us truth.

God is love, but teaching only the love of God misrepresents the character of God. God is forgiving, but teaching only forgiveness and not accountability leads people to believe a lie, giving them a license to sin. As a result, some will be fooled thinking they are truly redeemed and have no reason to change. But in the gospel of Matthew, Jesus said, "By their fruit you will recognize them" (7:16). To be blunt, this means that if neither God nor man can see a transformation in our lives, then there never was any transformation. And the person described here will be shocked and disappointed at the judgment to hear Jesus say, "Depart from Me, for I never knew you" (7:23).

To tell people they have time to consider salvation risks their very souls. What if they die having never accepted Christ? What if they get caught up in what they are doing and grow cold toward the things of God? Scripture says plainly that today is the day of salvation; not one of us is guaranteed tomorrow (2 Cor. 6:2; Matt. 25:13).

Second Peter 3:9–10 says this:

"The Lord isn't really being slow about his promise, as some people think. No, he is being patient for your sake. He does not want anyone to be destroyed, but wants everyone to repent. But the day of the Lord will come as unexpectedly as a thief. Then the heavens will pass away with a terrible noise, and the very elements themselves will disappear in fire, and the earth and everything on it will be found to deserve judgment" (NLT).

Leaders who teach only one perspective of God in hopes of increasing their membership, popularity and wealth are in no uncertain terms misleading followers down a broad path. On the other hand, good shepherds teach a balanced view of God, keeping his love, mercy, holiness, wrath and justice in mind. Leaving out any of these things jeopardizes the spiritual future of a pastor's flock, and the sheep's blood will, no doubt, be on his hands.

Chapter 11

# WHAT APPEARS TO BE TRUTH

A TEACHER MAY TEACH THE TRUTH NINETY-NINE PERCENT OF THE time, but we must remember that in God's eyes even a one percent error is still wrong and will be judged as sin. A teacher who refuses to preach the whole gospel but selectively preaches some things while ignoring others is in grave error. Truth demands complete, unadulterated loyalty to Scripture, with nothing added or subtracted, and anything else is suspect. John put it this way in Revelation 22:18–19:

> "For I testify to everyone who hears the words of the prophecy of this book: If anyone adds to these things, God will add to him the plagues that are written in this book, and if anyone takes away from the words of the book of this prophecy, God shall take away his part from the Book of Life, from the holy city, and from the things which are written in this book."

Often times, people accept what is mostly a true message from someone they love and respect, but they may wonder about a few of the finer points that sound questionable. After giving it some thought, even if they feel the message was wrong in some respect, they defer to leadership, believing they are trustworthy. Dr. Harry Ironside did not think this was a proper response:

> "Truth mixed with error is equivalent to all error, except that it is more innocent looking and, therefore, more dangerous. God hates such a mixture! Any error, or any truth-and-error mixture, calls for definite exposure and repudiation. To condone such is to be unfaithful to God and His Word and treacherous to imperiled souls for whom Christ died."

The whole truth is essential to our well-being. If I suffer with migraines, and my doctor says a pill was created to cure migraines, but fails to tell me that the side effects could kill me, he is not telling me the whole truth. It might be true it could stop my headaches, but withholding one small fact could cost me my life.

Some rat poisons are made up of ninety-eight percent cornmeal and two percent poison. And although the percentage of cornmeal far outweighs the poison, it is still a lethal combination—not exactly something anyone would want to use to fry chicken. The two percent is really the important ingredient because it makes the whole container deadly.

What if you opened a package of ham and found that two of the five slices were black with mold? Would you eat the other three? Not unless you have a death wish. But as believers, we often flock to those who are gifted speakers who reference Scriptures but are not always scriptural. Perhaps for the most part, they say things we can agree with, but there is also a flipside. For something to be sound teaching, it must be one-hundred percent scriptural.

Teachers often excuse error by saying, *"I'm only human and I, too, make mistakes."* While that is true and understandable, it is no excuse for teaching error. Teaching error is rarely a mistake but is usually deliberate. And while there are certain doctrinal distinctions because of denominational emphases and applications, there can be no mistaking doctrinal errors that disagree with Scripture.

God knows we are all human, but we must not teach others outside of the power and leading of the Holy Spirit. If we have submitted ourselves and asked the Lord to speak through us, laying aside our human opinions and preconceived notions, God will use us to teach things that are beyond our full comprehension. It is truly amazing!

If God intended for us to merely teach about self-help methods, he would have used the apostles to develop a psychologist's handbook. If he wanted the gospel to be totally academic, God would have inspired a theological textbook. But God did not choose these things to preach the gospel. His desire is for Christian leaders to commit themselves totally to the kingdom and to be passionate about one thing and one thing alone—teaching the salvation message and making disciples of God's people through the Holy Spirit's power and anointing. According to the Bible, anything else is "another gospel."

A word that is seldom mentioned from the pulpit anymore is *carnal*. It relates to what is fleshy and unspiritual. Romans 8:5–14 says:

"For those who live according to the flesh set their minds on the things of the flesh, but those who live according to the Spirit, the things of the Spirit. For to be carnally minded is death, but to be spiritually minded is life and peace. Because the carnal mind is enmity against God; for it is not subject to the law of God, nor indeed can be. So then, those who are in the flesh cannot please God. But you are not in the flesh but in the Spirit, if indeed the Spirit of God dwells in you. Now if anyone does not have the Spirit of Christ, he is not His. And if

Christ is in you, the body is dead because of sin, but the Spirit is life because of righteousness. But if the Spirit of Him who raised Jesus from the dead dwells in you, He who raised Christ from the dead will also give life to your mortal bodies through His Spirit who dwells in you. Therefore, brethren, we are debtors—not to the flesh, to live according to the flesh. For if you live according to the flesh you will die; but if by the Spirit you put to death the deeds of the body, you will live. For as many as are led by the Spirit of God, these are sons of God."

In other words, if we are dead to sin we will not continue to live as if nothing happened to change us. On the other hand, if we are alive to sin and enjoy it the way we always have, absolutely nothing happened to change us and we are unrepentant.

The church is not just supposed to be a place where we go to feel good. It is intended as a place to meet God, to hear God's Word, and to be transformed by the renewing of our minds—to be convicted, encouraged, healed and restored when we confess our sins and line up according to God's ways. The church is there to equip us to reach out and share the gospel with those who do not yet know our wonderful Lord.

It grieves my heart to know how the Word of God is so carelessly tossed around, and I mean that in the literal sense. Often times, people think the Bible is just another book. We toss them carelessly on the dashboards of our cars and even set them on our coffee tables so we can put coffee mugs on top of them. Let us keep in mind that the Bible truly is unique in the sense that it reveals the mind of God, what he thinks, how he feels, and everything about him. We should treat it with the respect it rightly deserves. It is the written, revealed Word that allows us to know who the Creator is.

If that is so, we must ask ourselves how can we know the

mind of God when we never crack open the Bible? How can we know the will of God when we scarcely know who he is? Many people miss God entirely because they rely on questionable leaders to teach them, rather than studying the Word for themselves. This is a very dangerous thing to do. The Bible says many shall be deceived by wolves in sheep's clothing. They are deleterious teachers who appear harmless, yet are anything but. Recently, I heard a story about how the Sioux Indians caught buffaloes. When hunting buffaloes, the Sioux learned not to approach the herd directly, for then they would run out of range of their spears. After many unsuccessful attempts, they came upon a plan that eventually worked with ease. The hunters wrapped themselves in the skin of an animal the buffaloes did not fear. Closer and closer they edged up to the unsuspecting herd. When close enough, they ripped off the animal skin and speared the buffalo in the heart.

This is tantamount to the strategy of Satan and his ministers who "come to you in sheep's clothing, but inwardly they are ferocious wolves" (Jesus' warning in Matt. 7:15). Sheep are fearful animals that run when they see wolves. Deadly teachers wrap themselves in sheep's clothing so they do not appear dangerous to the flock.

In Acts chapter 20, Paul told believers to remember his teachings and protective warnings so that they might not be scammed by deceptive teachers. He said, "Even from your own number men will arise and distort the truth in order to draw away disciples after them. So be on your guard!" (20:30–31). If people are not warned by true teachers, untruthful teachers may rob them of the truth they once held dear.

If a pastor taught the same message nonstop, even if that message was intended to protect his people, many might leave out of boredom (Phil. 3:1). A problem occurs when we become dissatisfied with the old and are always looking for something new. We leave in search of something that will move us emotionally, but we really starve for the truth that equips and protects us. It is in such churches that questionable teachers operate and thrive.

The books of Timothy and Titus are called Pastoral Epistles, which means they are books that are vital for spiritual leaders to know. In 1 Timothy chapter one, Paul, the apostolic father, is teaching his spiritual son, Timothy, who is about to begin pastoring the church in Ephesus. Paul spells out his concern regarding heretical teachers in the first eleven verses:

"Paul, an apostle of Jesus Christ, by the commandment of God our Savior and the Lord Jesus Christ, our hope, To Timothy, a true son in the faith: Grace, mercy, and peace from God our Father and Jesus Christ our Lord. As I urged you when I went into Macedonia—remain in Ephesus that you may charge some that they teach no other doctrine, nor give heed to fables and endless genealogies, which cause disputes rather than godly edification which is in faith. Now the purpose of the commandment is love from a pure heart, from a good conscience, and from sincere faith, rom which some, having strayed, have turned aside to idle talk, desiring to be teachers of the law, understanding neither what they say nor the things which they affirm. But we know that the law is good if one uses it lawfully, knowing this: that the law is not made for a righteous person, but for the lawless and insubordinate, for the ungodly and for sinners, for the unholy and profane, for murderers of fathers and murderers of mothers, for manslayers, for fornicators, for sodomites, for kidnappers, for liars, for perjurers, and if there is any other thing that is contrary to sound doctrine, according to the glorious gospel of the blessed God which was committed to my trust."

Paul urged Timothy to make sure the people were staying the course with sound doctrine and keeping within the parameters of God's Word. Many times, then and now, people claim to have a revelation from God that normally starts with, "The Lord told me," but the so-called revelation does not line up with Scripture. Any true revelation from the Redeemer must agree with what is already recorded in God's revealed Word. Any true insight from God will not contradict the written Word. Galatians 1:8 tells us that that no one, not even an angel, should be allowed to preach any gospel other than the one Paul preached straight from the Word. If that happens, he is to be accursed. This was such an important point that the apostle said it twice: "Even if we or an angel from heaven should teach a gospel other than the one we preached to you, let him be accursed! As we have already said, so now I say again: If anybody is preaching to you a gospel other than what you accepted, let him be accursed!" *If an angel has appeared to us in a dream, it is our responsibility to compare everything he says with Scripture. If the two do not agree, we must defer to the Bible every time. God will never direct anyone to do or say something that is contrary to the Word.* We can take that to the bank.

The prophet Ezekiel rebukes misleading shepherds and writes about how God commits himself to his flock:

"The message came to me from the LORD: "Son of man, prophesy against the shepherds, the leaders of Israel. Give them this message from the Sovereign LORD: Destruction is certain for you shepherds who feed yourselves instead of your flocks. Shouldn't shepherds feed their sheep? You drink the milk, wear the wool, and butcher the best animas, but you let your flocks starve. You have not taken care of the weak. You have not tended the sick or bound up the broken bones. You have not gone looking for those who have wandered away and are lost. Instead, you have ruled them with force and cruelty. So my sheep have been scattered without a shepherd. They are easy prey for any wild animal. They have wandered through the mountains and hills, across the face of the earth, yet not one has gone to search for them. Therefore, you shepherds, hear the word of the LORD: As surely as I live, says the Sovereign LORD, you abandoned my flock and left them to be attacked by every wild animal. Though you were my shepherds, you didn't search for my sheep when they were lost. You took care of yourselves and left the sheep to starve. Therefore, you shepherds, hear the word of the LORD. This is what the Sovereign LORD says: I now consider these shepherds my enemies, and I will hold them responsible for what has happened to my flock. I will take away their right to feed the flock, along with their right to feed themselves. I will rescue my flock from their mouths; the sheep will no longer be their prey" (34:1–10 NLT).

God is saying the time has come for him to turn things around. Enough is enough! These greedy leaders have made an entire living by devouring God's people, taking the best of the fat and wool, and leaving them with nothing. And all this is done while they are asking for more!

How will God turn things around? By causing his people to flee such teachers. He will release his flock from supporting such teachers by hindering their supporters so they can no longer financially give. Ezekiel says:

"And the word of the Lord came to me, saying, "Son of man, prophesy against the prophets of Israel who prophesy out of their own heart, "Hear the word of the Lord! Thus says the Lord God: 'Woe to the foolish prophets, who follow their own spirit and have seen nothing! O Israel, your prophets are like foxes in the deserts. You have not gone up into the gaps to build a wall for the house of Jerusalem to stand in battle on the day of the Lord. They have envisioned futility and false divination, saying, 'Thus says the Lord!' But the Lord has not sent them; yet they hope that the word may be confirmed. Have you not seen a futile vision, and have you not spoken false divination? You say, 'The Lord says,' but I have not spoken. Therefore, thus says the Lord God: 'Because you have spoken nonsense and envisioned lies, therefore I am indeed against you," says the Lord God. My hand will be against the prophets who envision futility and who divine lies; they shall not be in the assembly of My people nor be written in the record of the house of Israel, nor shall they enter into the land of Israel. Then you shall know that I am the Lord God, because, they have seduced My people saying, 'Peace' when there is no peace. . . . Therefore thus says the Lord God: "I will cause a stormy wind to break forth in My fury; and there shall be flooding rain in My anger, and great hailstones in fury to consume it. . . . With the lies you have made the heart of the righteous sad, whom I have not made sad, and you have strengthened the hands of the wicked so that he does not turn from his wicked way to save his life. Therefore you shall no longer envision futility nor practice divination; for I will deliver My people out of your hand, and you shall know that I am the Lord" (13:1–10, 13, 22).

It is clear God takes prophecy very seriously, and so should those who claim to speak for him. If a pastor or teacher presents something contrary to God's Word, or consistently prophesies things that do not manifest, we are to shake the dust off our shoes and leave them. God is not in it.

Nor will God change his mind and suggest we do something this year that he forbade us doing last year. Anyone having a dream contradicting what Scripture says to do or not do can be assured God is not behind it.

When church leaders begin straying off the mark, they often do questionable things they would never have approved of before. Perhaps they now preach on something they preached against earlier. That has been the case with many leaders who have had affairs with other women in the church, or divorced their wives to marry someone younger or someone who supports their false teaching. They may excuse it by saying, "The Lord told me," "God said it was no problem," or "God knows my heart." But do not be deceived by these kinds of men; no matter how respected they are or how large or successful their ministries appear to be. These things are an abomination to the Lord, and it is time for godly people to move on.

Some leaders change the Word to suit the people's attitudes and prejudices. It is not, however, their prerogative to dilute or alter the teaching of Scripture. In fact, real spiritual leaders should not concern themselves with the opinions of those who will not tolerate sound doctrine. We must continue to preach God's Word in the context in which it was written, and we must do so to whoever has ears to hear. To water down the Bible is to elevate the people over God, which is no different than setting up idols for worship. The first of the Ten Commandments says, "You shall have no other gods before me" (Ex. 20:3).

God's standards never change. He is not a pragmatist, and he is not a situational ethicist. He does not act according to what the circumstances dictate. Those who practice such things believe that if they cannot figure something out or if they do not want to figure it out, then either they have misunderstood or it cannot be of God. They surmise that when something does not fit their own notion of things or their personal opinion on things that it cannot be of God. This is false from beginning to end and can't be further from the truth. God demands our obedience, whether we agree with something or not.

Deuteronomy 4:1–2 reads:

> "And now, Israel, listen carefully to these laws and regulations that I am about to teach you. Obey them so that you may live, so you may enter and occupy the land the Lord, the God of your ancestors, is giving you. Do not add to or subtract from these commands I am giving you from the Lord your God. Just obey them."

This Scripture can be supported with Proverbs 30:5, which reads, "Every word of God is pure; He is a shield to those who put their trust in Him. Do not add to His words, lest He rebuke you, and you be found a liar."

Scriptures must be supported by other Scriptures, which mean we must never build a doctrine off a single verse. Neither can we say whatever we want and then pray for God to back us up. We cannot expect the Lord to support us and give us whatever we want when we go against what he has already decreed. That is just never going to happen.

For example, some church leaders excuse their sins by saying that a "generational curse" keeps them bound, leaving them with no other choice. They hide behind the teaching of inherited guilt. But Ezekiel 18:4 says, "The soul who sins is the one who will die." Pure and simple. There is no excuse for sin when God has offered to set us free to live in righteousness.

When we sin—for any reason—we alone must stand in judgment, not our parents or forefathers. The truth is that books make money for authors who excuse sin due to generational curses. Undiscerning readers buy the books and then buy into the false argument. But if a doctor said we have high blood pressure, which could be hereditary, we would try getting rid of the problem rather than blaming it on something generational. *Why would we agree with a generational sin but refuse to accept a generational illness?*

The problem with heresy—a self-willed opinion that takes the place of an absolute truth—is not that people reject the entire gospel, but they selectively choose what they want to believe and reject the rest. This is dangerous ground, very much like walking on thin ice. How far can one go before breaking the ice and drowning? God requires us to believe all or nothing. There are absolutely no gray areas. Either we take him at his Word, or we do not. Unfortunately, this is exactly the way some teachers teach, picking and choosing what they will believe.

In the case of generational curses (which, by the way, is one of the most popular messages today in some circles), pastors should teach the truth that salvation breaks every single generational penalty. And while we may have spiritual weaknesses that remain after certain curses are broken, we have supernatural power (the Holy Spirit) to resist such temptations. The salient point is that we are responsible for the choices we make, and if we sin, we must confess it, repent and go in the other direction. God is a forgiving God, but this does not mean we have a license or an excuse to continue to sin. Paul made it clear that being justified does not give anyone permission to forsake morality: "What then? Shall we sin because we are not under law but under grace? God forbid" (Rom. 6:15 ).

It is true that God told Ezekiel there were consequences we may have to endure because of the sins of our parents, but that does not mean we must fall into the same sin. In fact, if we sin in the same way our parents did, we must take responsibility for our behavior, for Scripture says God will judge us for what *we* did in the flesh.

Chapter 12

# THE TRUTH ABOUT THE PROSPERITY GOSPEL

IN NEW TESTAMENT TIMES NEARLY ALL THOSE IN THE JEWISH community believed the scribes and Pharisees were right, that is until Jesus showed up and contradicted such a notion. Why didn't Jesus expose the Pharisees error far earlier than he did? The answer is that God will never expose error until he has a replacement (a true shepherd). But know this, when the Lord begins shining a light and exposing error, it is time for things to change.

When Jesus arrived on the scene in Israel, he upset the apple cart. He turned the status quo upside down with a new truth to replace the old error. He taught his disciples and the people who followed a new way to live. He also taught them how to replace the old system of things. It is encouraging to know that God never leaves us out on a limb without leadership. But in this case, the new leadership stayed undercover until the time was right for it to be revealed.

In the gospel of Matthew, Jesus made a statement that may be easily misunderstood. He said, "I tell you that unless your righteousness surpasses that of the Pharisees and the teachers of the law, you will not enter the kingdom of heaven" (5:20). What did he mean? He meant that though the Pharisees and scribes were in positions of leadership, their righteousness was still as filthy rags—and no different from anyone else's. In essence, he was saying that it wasn't their leadership or feigned righteousness that would get them into heaven, but rather pure hearts, which they did not have. Clearly, Jesus upset the party line in his day, and he is still doing that today.

In our day, the party line is called the "prosperity gospel." And though we have alluded to this earlier, it is important to put this thinking into perspective. The gospel of prosperity is a gospel of health and wealth, for it teaches that those who give generously should expect a financial reward. It also teaches that, in fact, God wants everyone to be rich. All one has to do is claim great wealth for themselves. This is equivalent to going around, claiming things in Jesus' name, as if one is rubbing a rabbit's foot or saying a magic incantation. Some people call this the "Name-It-and-Claim-It" movement. You simply name it, and in Christ's name claim it. But any resemblance the prosperity gospel or name-it-and-claim-it gospel has to the actual Word of God is merely coincidental.

There were many instances in Scripture where God's people suffered poverty, or at least the normal financial ups and downs that transpire with life's circumstances. Even Paul mentioned being content in whatever situation he faced. He said, "I know what it is to be in need, and I know what it is to have plenty. I have learned the secret of being content in any and every situation, whether well fed or hungry, whether living in plenty or in want" (Phil. 4:12).

The prosperity gospel is heresy. Such things are not of God, and they have nothing to do with real faith. Real faith is only as good as the person on whom it rests—and it should rest on Jesus Christ, not on one's concern for their own welfare.

Of course it is true that Scripture tells us to pray for the healing of the sick and pray in faith for what we need, but if our motives are wrong and if we merely want these things to satisfy our own lusts, we are in error and must not expect God to approve. To expect otherwise is to change God's intent for faith into an idol that we worship, no different than the Israelites' golden calf.

This name-it-and-claim-it philosophy originally began as a deviation from what God had said about faith. In time, however, it took the slippery slope down into greater liberties with the truth, until it became a full-blown heresy. Along the way, New Age doctrines (weird alternative approaches to spirituality) also crept in, until finally it bore no similarity to Christian doctrine or to what God had already revealed about faith.

Among some of the doctrines that make up the prosperity gospel fraud is one called *positive confession*. This actually demands that we deny the truth of what is happening. For example: "Do you have weak eyesight and have to wear eyeglasses? Do you want to get rid of the glasses? Then simply positively confess that you have been healed and that you now have 20/20 vision. If it does not immediately appear that you have perfect vision, it is a trick of Satan, trying to convince you that you have not been healed. Just use positive confession."

As believers, we must realize that true faith never denies fact. Faith treats fact like the reality it is and submits it to God, who can then do something to change it, should that be in his will. Everything we believe must revolve around the will of God and the exaltation of Jesus Christ. In order to be truly his, we must submit our hearts, become servants of God and trust him to work out all the details of our lives. Certainly we must ask the Lord for what we need, but we must do it with humble hearts, not demanding what we want, when and how we want it. If we demand things and call those demands "faith," I can say without a doubt that we should examine our hearts to see if we really belong to Jesus.

If we, as believers, ask for wisdom regarding our physical needs, we may be led to seek a doctor's care rather than a miraculous healing. Only God knows why this would be— maybe he will use our witness in one way or another to minister to people.

The "father" of the Word of Faith movement was Kenneth Hagin, an influential Pentecostal preacher. After hearing his charismatic teaching, many rushed to get on the bandwagon to teach such a message. Over time, however, Hagin wrote in his last book, *"The Midas Touch,"* that he realized the voice of the Holy Spirit was rebuking him for teaching such outright error. Being obedient, he went to his followers—leaders in the movement—and confessed his error, only to have his confession rejected by many. The vast majority of the people in the outrageous Word of Faith movement did not want to stop preaching and teaching the doctrines taught to them by Hagin. As with most things, it all came down to money. The prosperity gospel taught by Hagin and his crowd was raking in big bucks, lavish lifestyles and private jets for those who preached it.

If we actually study Scripture, we see that the gospel never promises we will all be rich. There have always been people in every socioeconomic group who loved the Lord. Scripture goes so far as to say that the poor will always be with us. Then how can they, in good conscience, preach that God will give us all great wealth?

The problem comes in how we define the word *rich*. In human terms, it means finances that allow a person to buy what they want without counting the cost. In God's kingdom, however, the term *rich* means a wide range of other things. It means blessed in terms of faith, friends, loved ones and abundance in wisdom and knowledge of God. Often, the word means everything *but* money from God's point of view, partly because he knows money can totally destroy our relationship with him. It happens all the time.

Some believers have the gift of giving (Rom. 12:8). They always have what they need with a surplus for the purpose of giving to promote the preaching of the gospel. There will be some who have just what they need, and no more. Then, others will have barely enough to meet their needs. Because God has not promised us all material wealth, we dare not risk what resources we have to invest in get-rich-quick schemes and questionable multi-level marketing programs, even when the church promotes them. *They are never legitimate.* Pyramid schemes (multi-level marketing or Ponzi scheme swindles) only benefit the people at the very top. The rest are cheated and almost always lose most, if not all, of their investment.

These schemes would never appeal to us if we were not at least a little greedy. The same can be said of the prosperity gospel. In the end, vying for wealth every waking hour robs us of our time and attention to God, and that in itself is enough reason to refuse such blab-it-and-grab-it teaching (Prov. 15:27).

## THE AMERICAN GOSPEL VS. THE GOSPEL OF CHRIST

Although God is raising up true leaders to expose corruption in the church and to free people from erroneous teaching, many false teachers' followers will become offended that someone is messing with their idols.

Besides Washington, D.C., the church is the only other place where lawbreakers can hide out and be protected. Only in these two places can leaders run crooked operations while the people applaud them. But it is time to face the facts that these leaders are crooks and con artists. They are wolves who have honed the art of making their schemes look real.

Take the Ponzi scheme, for example. Here there is one person at the top, and under this person are several investors. The top three or four investors boast that their portfolios have tripled. However, those claims are made to give the scheme credibility so they can trick others into signing up. If no one bragged that he or she received a big windfall on one's money, others wouldn't join, and the whole scheme would fall. Take note of this: *Beware of leaders using their influence to promote investment opportunities to their followers. These situations rarely turn out profitable for the people; the leader is usually the only one who will see a return, and that's because he used his authority, along with "success" stories of others, along with false prophetic promises spoken openly to convince others to join him.* This is similar to schemes in today's church where the leaders are the only ones who seem to have testimonies. They are boasting about the blessings they claim came are a result of their sacrificial giving and their business investments. The hope is that they can bilk money from members who want the same blessings.

If something is the truth it should work for everyone across the board. If something works for only one or two, it is not the truth; it is not the gospel of Jesus Christ. The problem is that we have confused the American gospel of greed with Jesus' gospel. The Jesus that is preached on South Beach in Miami, Florida, should be the same Jesus that is preached in the jungles of Africa. The true gospel message never changes.

The American gospel cannot be preached in other countries because it teaches that God's love and approval can only be measured by the size of one's material possessions. That just does not work anywhere else. The American gospel says you are not saved unless you have a certain level of success and wealth. But that is not the gospel of Jesus Christ! How can that be the true gospel when there are people in other countries who love Jesus but sleep on dirt floors, with scarcely enough to eat?

The American gospel, as you might imagine, is constantly changing, depending on which way the wind is blowing. Years ago, we heard we weren't blessed if we lived in an apartment, because God wanted everyone to own a house. There is nothing wrong with owning a home, but such ownership is not a guarantee for everyone; therefore, it is wrong to make a doctrine out of it. But unwise people, who lack spiritual understanding, will walk around a house seven times, throwing oil and claiming a property "In Jesus' name" with a credit score of 500. Such people are clearly not in any position for home ownership because they have not learned to handle their finances wisely.

People go through seasons of life, and sometimes they are still growing and not yet wise enough for certain things. Who would give their child a car just because he or she demands one? Likewise, God does not give us everything we demand. There are some things we desire that we are not spiritually mature for. And yet the prosperity movement has made a doctrine out of something God did not intend. And because of such destructive teaching, many who could not afford their expensive homes are now losing them to foreclosure.

Not surprisingly, that teaching has now morphed, and home ownership is not enough anymore. Now to be really blessed our homes have to be paid off. And while there is nothing intrinsically wrong with wanting to be debt-free, the hireling has an ulterior motive for preaching such things. And again it has to do with greed. He knows that everyone who owns a home wishes to be debt-free from their mortgage, and they will be able to give more to his ministry if they are free from paying their mortgage.

Recently, some hirelings have encouraged people to give large sums as "seed money" when asking God for a house or asking that a house be brought out of foreclosure. On the envelope, people are told to write the word "house" and place it on the altar. And guess where that money goes? They might even invite a well-known "prophet" to confirm that you will have your house within ninety days. This prophet gives the hireling's word (but not God's word) creditability.

The hireling is not finished, however. If we want to be debt-free, we must sow more money. It is an ever-evolving game where the rules are always changing so the covetous leader can get rich.

## ACCOUNTABILITY OF LEADERS

It is mind-blowing to witness so many people who think they are serving God while sitting under the teaching of a dishonest hireling. One of the reasons such behavior continues in the church is because we have not held our leaders accountable or demand that they teach sound doctrine. The list of dishonest hirelings would be very long, and so would the list be of fraudulent shepherds who have been caught in their greed and run out of the ministry.

The sad truth is, because we have settled for watered-down sermons that entertain us but do not challenge us, we have no good foundation from which to operate. Few talk about holiness anymore, or heaven, or hell or the blood of Christ. Such topics are no fun. If we are not trained in the Word, there is no way we can discern whether a message is coming from God or the Devil.

Many of us believe all we need for discernment is the Holy Spirit. But remember, our hearts and minds are deceitful and desperately wicked above all things (Jer. 17:9). This makes it essential that we constantly renew our minds to line up with the heart of God.

Paul's instructions in 2 Timothy 2:15 teach us to "Do your best to present yourself to God as one approved, a workman who does not need to be ashamed and who correctly handles the word of truth." This implies that if we do not present ourselves to God as workmen who correctly handle Scripture, we will be ashamed, embarrassed, empty and cheated. We simply will not be on top of our game.

Soon the day is coming when God will strip away all the superficial things (gigantic choirs, large orchestras and all other entertainment) and eventually we will have to face the truth— our leaders have done very little to prepare us to meet him. *Shocking!* We will have to face the truth, although few will be prepared to do so. The reason some cannot handle this truth is because we are too prideful to accept that we and our leaders have been wrong. Truth demands a response. Once it has been revealed, we must admit we are wrong, and we must change direction.

What will we do once God turns on the light, illuminating truth so we can see we have been wrong? Will we rejoice that the Lord has given us one more chance to change, or will we be paralyzed by shame and guilt? Will we grow stubborn and resistant to leaving our unsound doctrine behind? Or will we exclaim with excitement, "One thing I do know. I was blind but now I see!" (John 9:25). Understanding that we could have died in our sins but God extended mercy should make us leap for joy and praise the Lord our Savior!

The reality about the prosperity gospel is that it is not true. If we fail to demand that teachers teach us truth and if we fail to study to show ourselves approved, we will fall for anything. The right way for our leaders to behave is seen in the first letter of Peter:

> "The elders who are among you I exhort, I who am a fellow elder and a witness of the sufferings of Christ, and also a partaker of the glory that will be revealed. Shepherd the flock

of God which is among you, serving as overseers, not by compulsion but willingly, not for dishonest gain, but eagerly. Nor as being lords over those entrusted to you, but being examples to the flock" (5:1–3).

Verse two represents hirelings, but the third verse represents dictators, which we will discuss next. Peter tells shepherds to be certain they are not leading because of the temptation for dishonest gain—money. As the gospel of Matthew clearly shows, a true shepherd will have compassion for his sheep:

"Then Jesus went about all the cities and villages, teaching in their synagogues, preaching the gospel of the kingdom, and healing every sickness and every disease among the people. But when He saw the multitudes He was moved with compassion for them, because they were weary and scattered, like sheep having no shepherd. Then He said to His disciples, "The harvest truly is plentiful, but the laborers are few. Therefore pray the Lord of harvest to send out laborers into His harvest" (9:35–38).

Jesus was grieved because he felt compassion for the crowds. Note verse 36 in the New Living Translation:

"When he saw the crowds, he had compassion on them because they were confused and helpless, like sheep without a shepherd."

These people had spiritual leadership, but it was bad leadership. Therefore, it resulted in their being harassed, distressed, bewildered and helpless. This is what dangerous teachers do, and when we follow them, sooner or later we end up suffering and saying, "God, this can't be You." We will be robbed of our strength, our motivation and our passion for God. We will then ask the question, "Why would he allows such things to happen in his house?" But God is not to blame. This is a wake-up call for those of us who are listening.

One dead giveaway to being harassed by such leaders is when we dread going to church. It is bad enough when we have to face our day-to-day problems, but it is adding insult to injury to have to face an unbiblical teacher on Sunday. We begin anticipating stress and strife at church until we hate seeing Sunday arrive. These things grieved Jesus in his day, and they still grieve him today.

Jesus warned that it is better for us to be thrown into the sea with a millstone tied around our necks than to cause the innocent to suffer (Luke 17:2). This comment still applies today. Prosperity preachers may think that because God has been silent they are getting away with their false teaching. But God is saying "enough is enough."

He will no longer tolerate those who teach lies from the pulpit, and he is now shaking and judging the household of faith. Will we stand or fall under such scrutiny?

Chapter 13

# DICTATORS

*DISCLAIMER:* GOD HAS NOT RELEASED THIS MESSAGE TO BE MEAN or vindictive. He is releasing it to let his people know he has had enough. He wants us to be free to worship him in spirit and in truth during these last days. To that end he wants to equip us to discern the difference between true shepherds and untruthful teachers.

Who are the dictators? Simply put, dictators are those leaders who desire for people to worship them. Their agenda is all about control. Dictators rise up from within the church, assume leadership positions and teach things that take people's eyes off Christ to focus instead on them. They initially preach what people want to hear to gain popularity, and over time they begin feeling they personally have a right to tell people how to live, apart from what the Holy Spirit himself has to say on the subject. Eventually, they will have an opinion on every aspect of someone's life, and they will make the sheep feel as if they are not capable of managing their own affairs. They freely give advice, often using the word "should."

Dictators will meddle in the personal affairs of their flock when it is none of their business. They often assume a very unhealthy role in advising how to spend money, who to marry, where to live, who to associate with, how to spend spare time and what positions to take in church. The list goes on and on. This is not to say that God will not give a godly pastor sound wisdom for our personal lives. The question would be, is it godly wisdom?

When intruding into the personal lives of their flock, dictators take the place of the Holy Spirit, misrepresent Christ and frequently leave people in despair and hopelessness. And what is worse, their victims feel like God is responsible for their injuries.

## Touch Not My Anointed

A friend told me this about his bad experience with a dictator whose main goal was to use fear and false curses to control people:

> "He claimed that the only people who were saved were those who followed him. He caused division everywhere he went and even attempted to destroy my marriage. He was especially gifted in locating someone who was more loyal to him than to their family, and then he would turn them against their spouses and family. He stressed accountability and submission to him, while the only person he submitted to was himself. According to this dictator, one was either supporting him and his vision or one was being used by the Devil. Predicatively, his favorite Scripture was, "Touch not my anointed, do my prophets no harm" (Ps. 105:15). I thank God for giving me the strength and wisdom to leave this false prophet."

Over time it is possible that a hireling will become a dictator, although some leaders will remain hirelings and will never be anything else. Some leaders are strictly dictators; they start as dictators, and they end the same way. If a hireling does not get what he wants voluntarily, he can begin demanding it and transform into a dictator. In the book of Micah chapter 3, the prophets prophesied peace for those who fed them and war for those who did not (v. 5). In other words, if the people lavished them with good things, they prophesied flattering words over their lives. But if they failed to give them what they wanted, the prophets spoke curses against them. This is exactly how church dictators operate today.

Dictators are dangerous leaders. In chapter 34 of Ezekiel, the prophet says the leaders used cruelty to rule the people. They neglected the sheep and they ruled harshly and brutally. This is the way of church dictators; they always harm their people. They control them by playing mind games and using reverse psychology. They use double-talk and always blame the people when things go wrong. Their victims can never leave the ministry without their blessing. There are always negative consequences to associating with a dictator. God is against these dictators and will hold them accountable.

### SERVING UNDER A DICTATOR

One woman told me this about serving under a dictator:

"Though I was under a dictator, I didn't know it at the time. I knew something was not right; therefore, I began to pray and ask God to open my eyes so I could see. This changed my life forever! I began seeing so clearly how the pastor was using me to make others do things in the church. For example, I had just begun serving in the church when the pastor stood me up in front of everybody and said I was on fire for God, and even though I had just arrived, I did not mind working for God. As you can imagine, this caused great jealousy and division between me and others. For a time I was also part of the dance team, but there were so many control issues that I finally stopped going to church except occasionally. God finally gave me a sign that I was to stop going entirely, so I wrote a letter saying I would not be returning but that I was grateful for all I had learned.

I got a phone call once the pastor received the letter, and that was the beginning of my nightmare. The pastor challenged my decision to leave and tried to change my mind. When I returned to the church for a baby christening, she preached at me publicly so that everyone knew it was me she spoke about. She even went so far as to give me a "Word from the Lord" that I had not been released to leave because I belonged to her. Then she said if I lived without her covering, death and destruction would come upon me, and she gave me a scarf for protection.

Once I understood the truth about this dictator, I told my friends and family I was no longer growing there and that God had released me—and if they felt the same way they should seek God's face and follow him, as well. Soon they began leaving, too. It did not take long for the pastor to call me and leave messages and texts on my phone. She said I was trying to destroy her ministry and that she would make me pay. She used the usual verse, 'Touch not God's anointed, and do his prophet no harm.' Then she began spreading rumors about me and another person who left the church, and she caused deep division in my home and with my family. That pastor persecuted and afflicted my life! It was a nightmare from hell, and I would have thought it was all a dream had I not lived through it myself. I can only thank God for rescuing me."

## SIGNS THAT IDENTIFY DICTATORS

- Dictators never allow people to leave their ministry in peace.
- Dictators love to have control over everything and everyone.
- Dictators often use humiliation to keep people in line.
- Dictators teach frequently from Hebrews 13:17, "Obey your leaders and submit to their authority." Every message reflects back to the issue of authority and submission.
- Dictators teach that God will only bless you if you submit to *their* authority. And while it is a good thing to submit to God, it is a dangerous thing to submit to a dictator.
- Dictators show favoritism in the church. They love for people to compete for their attention and approval. Whoever serves them best will be recognized and rewarded, putting people against each other within the body of Christ. Dictators flourish when there is strife in the church because they are the center of all the attention.
- Dictators spend time only with those who agree with them. They are very insecure and only feel secure as long as they have control. They do not exercise patience with people who refuse to cater to their egos.
- Dictators become furious when someone leaves the church. The offender's name is made public from the pulpit in order to instill fear in those who remain. They will often go as far as to speak curses over the "errant one."
- And worst of all, such leaders teach the people that

they cannot hear God or succeed in life apart from them.

- Dictators often use spiritual gifts to divide or promote fear. They say things like, "God told me to tell you that you will die if you leave," or "God has not released you yet."
- Dictators will always divide households.

The Enemy often raises up dictators in the church in order to manipulate and control God's people. But keep in mind that God never gave a man or a woman the authority to have dominion over other people (2 Cor. 1:24). Consider this quote by Abraham Lincoln: "Nearly all men can stand adversity, but if you want to test a man's character, give him power." The proof of character is evident in what a person does with power. If that power changes him, there is something in his character that is not right. Leonard Ravenhill once said, "Everyone wants to be clothed with power but no one wants to be stripped of self." Being stripped of oneself is an unknown reality for any dictator, for the hardest person for him to overcome is himself, because that's the last person who he believes is the problem.

Several years ago, there was something called the "shepherd's doctrine," which dictated that the sheep had to be under the care of a shepherd in order to be protected. This is where the concept of "covering" originated. Under this teaching, God's people were encouraged to find covering, lest God, in his righteousness, should grow angry and kill them in judgment for sin. Instead of teaching the people to repent and have faith in God, they taught that the human shepherd (teacher) was to be that covering. This gave the teacher much more power than God ever intended. And often that power was abused.

Today, this shepherd's doctrine teaching has resurfaced in a teaching called "kingdom dominion," which is best defined as a misinterpretation of the kingdom of God message, and it is the driving force behind many church dictators. They use their authority and influence to threaten and curse the people instead of loving them with the tender—but at times even tough—love of God. Such treatment encourages an unhealthy submission to leadership. In fact, this stifling environment is so overwhelming that people often feel unable to hear from God, unable to discern God's will and incapable of ruling their own spirits.

I believe in the local church. I pastor one in Miami, Florida. But I have learned that there is a very fine line between a true shepherd and a spiritual dictator. Many master manipulators hide their true motivation until their victims are deeply involved and badly wounded, some even emotionally scarred for life. A true shepherd will speak the truth in love, but for a dictator, control is the only issue. A good shepherd will protect without coercion and lead without domination.

Individuals are deeply impacted by the actions of dictators, and the type of personality the individual has seems to make little difference. Because certain teachings have been drilled into their minds and spirit, many people feel powerless to leave the dominance of the dictator, believing the teacher is equal with God and thinking God will be angry if they attempt escape. And though they can conclude that such teaching is wrong, they are often far too paralyzed by fear to leave.

In fact, insecurity is the underlying emotion motivating a dictator. It is said that even Adolf Hitler was driven by fear and doubt. Dictators struggle deeply with rejection; this is one reason they seek to control every circumstance. Their entire self-image rests upon the adoration and adulation of their followers, and any attempt for people to escape their clutches ignites fury in them. Mark this down: Every dictator suffers from a narcissistic personality disorder. They stress and demand loyalty, but yet, are incapable of reciprocating loyalty because they bleed insecurity.

Their deep insecurity dilemma is why they surround themselves with people who are incompetent and struggle with identity issues; for the dictator knows these type of people will show "great loyalty" to the person who made them feel validated and loved. It's called an "emotional love trap." The controller elevates the victim into a position of importance, even though they are not qualified to be in position, or showers the victim with great praise among others to psychologically trap the victim. The dictator believes by granting the individual this authority that they don't deserve, when it's time for the dictator to make unethical and unbiblical demands, the victim will feel compelled to agree or to oblige. The dictator knows that if he can appeal to the victim's sense of loyalty, gratitude and false love, he can carry out whatever his heart chooses.

Spiritual dictators are also threatened when people question their leadership (John 9:13–34). To question the leadership of a dictator is like asking if they are truly called and anointed by God. Such a question is intolerable to dictators. Many have unresolved emotional wounds, and while they constantly preach healing and deliverance to their flock, they themselves have not been healed or delivered.

## A TRAVESTY AND A SHAME

Here is an account of one man and his family leaving a dictator's ministry:

> "This written testimony is very real and dear to us, because of what we once believed and what we were subjected to. Our background is the Pentecostal Deliverance movement, where the leader is deemed 'higher' than the people, and where the spiritual gifts are more highly esteemed than the understanding and teaching of sound biblical doctrine. I say higher in the

sense that the leader has a significant amount of influence on individuals' faith, gifts, decisions, and so on. My wife and I were loyal members and held on to every word the leader spoke. He always said that he didn't have to say, 'thus says the Lord....' to be speaking under the divine inspiration of God. The church had an atmosphere dominated by fear, self-exaltation, and intimidation. In addition, because his instructions were considered to be from the Lord, questioning the leader was considered stiff-necked and rebellious.

During the middle of 2007, we became weary of the ministry, and our zeal for the Lord was decreasing. This stemmed from the nonsense and politics of the church, coupled with the 'vision of man.' This caused us to seek the Lord for direction because it was quickly becoming apparent that it was time for us to leave. However, before we left, my wife and I invited another ministry to ours and put together a youth revival in the hope that God would do something great. A couple of weeks prior to that event, we decided to remove a few of the youth leaders from staff due to lack of effort on their part. Ironically, the pastor (we still hadn't left the church at this time) assigned me the job of eliminating those who were out of line, not knowing that his son and daughter-in-law were among those who would be asked to leave. Right before the event the pastor said he had reinstated all those who had been dismissed. All of this after he had given me the go-ahead. So after the event I went to him and another pastor and announced my resignation as youth director. He responded that because I was a college student my focus was not where it should have been. The associate pastor pleaded with me to stay on as director and promised that everything would be all right. In that moment I knew the pastor was off base with God and his 'gifted' perceptions.

In the month of May of 2008, we finally decided to leave

the ministry. I spoke with the pastor on three separate occasions after our announcement, and his response was to belittle and intimidate us. He regaled me with all the things that were wrong with us. He said we were in the flesh and we were going to suffer shipwreck. He said he could control me if it was not for my wife. I was told my ministry would soon be nonexistent apart from him. We were sowing discord, he told me, by simply telling people we were leaving his ministry. According to him even my mother should not have heard from us that we were leaving. When I told him that I was previously afraid of him, he responded by saying that it was the anointing that I feared.

I praise the Lord for delivering us from that place. We didn't know what we got into initially. All we wanted to do was to serve the Lord with our whole hearts. Even now, some of the members are afraid to speak to us lest they end up disobeying their pastor. It is a travesty and a shame before God."

In order to worship in spirit and in truth, we must have the freedom to exalt God rather than a human, and when that is not possible because of a dictator such as the one just discussed, it is time to shake the dust off our feet and leave.

Jeremiah 23:1–4 speaks harshly regarding dictators:

"What sorrow awaits the leaders of my people—the shepherds of my sheep—for they have destroyed and scattered the very ones they were expected to care for," says the Lord. Therefore, this is what the Lord, the God of Israel, says to these shepherds: "Instead of caring for my flock and leading them to safety, you have deserted them and driven them to destruction. Now I will pour out judgment on you for the evil you have done to them. But I will gather together the remnant of my flock from the countries where I have driven them. I will bring them back to their own sheepfold, and they will be fruitful and increase in number. Then I will appoint responsible shepherds who will care for them, and they will never be afraid again. Not a single one will be lost or missing. I, the Lord, have spoken" (NLT).

Building upon what we have learned about the characteristics of church dictators, it is easy to understand how spurious religious cults originate. The word *cult* has been used so frequently that its true definition has been misconstrued. What I mean by the term *cult* is a group gathering together in an intense devotion around a specific person's misinterpretation or denial of essential biblical doctrines. Dictators gradually isolate victims from outside influences and end up exerting intense control over every aspect of their lives. Many cult leaders start out preaching the true Word of God, but they become consumed with the idea of power, influence and wealth. The cult group itself is the culmination of a dictator's search for adoration. Cult leaders demand complete loyalty and submission to the rules and restrictions they have laid out, and their rules and restrictions are always far more stringent than anything God asks. Anything less results in severe punishment, public humiliation and a loss of privileges.

Some cult members even lose their lives when the leader decides to make an example of them. They find out too late that they are trapped with absolutely no way out. Many of those who do find a way out never recover from post-traumatic stress and struggle to resume any kind of normal life. As a result of brainwashing, the members also have a distorted idea of what a father is and have a hard time relating to the concept of a loving God.

. . .

## THE INFLUENCE OF FALSE PROPHETS

A friend has offered this statement about the influence of a false prophet:

"Not too long after leaving the ministry where the pastor was a hireling, I became really good friends with a young woman whose husband was a 'prophet.' In the past, I had seen him move in the prophetic way, and he had been on target regarding past and current things. But he was way off when it came to future things. One day he prayed for me while I was pregnant and told me that I would be having a boy. He said this boy would be like Joab in the Bible. Because I was unfamiliar with Scripture, I believed everything he said. However, when I went for my doctor's appointment to learn the gender of my baby, the ultrasound tech said I was having a girl. I was surprised, and didn't want to believe it because I believed the prophet to be a "reliable" man of God who would never lie to me. Wanting a second opinion, I asked for another ultrasound, and the second also confirmed that it was a girl. A few days later I went to visit my friend and her husband, the prophet. As I was waiting for her, he asked me, 'If you have a girl, exactly what do you think that means?'

I told him, 'I guess I disobeyed God, so perhaps he was disappointed with me.' And he nodded his head yes. Also, he told me to divorce my husband because my husband saw through many of his schemes and would never really listen to him. Because I was very loyal and respected this prophet, he wanted me to get rid of my husband so I would remain loyal to him. Needless to say, almost eight years later my husband and I are still married, and we no longer sit under this man's false teaching.

Sitting under both a hireling and dictator robbed me of my passion and zeal to trust true shepherds. I lost every ounce of passion for God because of all the hurt I experienced. Now I am under a true shepherd whose desire is to feed God's sheep and point us in the right direction to be part of a great work that God destined for us. Just recently my pastor preached a sermon about the church of Ephesus, and how they lost their passion. When I asked God to help me understand why I lost my passion, he led me back to the original problem of sitting under the dictator and hireling. I am grateful to be free today and plan to do all I can to help others in the same situation."

Many times, dictators know the truth, but they have learned how to twist it to their own advantage. The reason these people are so dangerous is that they control people by mixing truth with error. They know enough truth to seem believable but are filled with enough error that makes them lethal. They are the ones who teach accountability, but it's usually out of the context of Scripture, and they are accountable to no one.

Dictators always try to coax personal details from their people that can be used to manipulate. This is a blatant misuse of power, far from God's original intent. In the end, it is clearly a type of spiritual abuse that God abhors. The best response is to turn and flee from these dishonorable shepherds.

Chapter 14

# IT'S TIME TO DECIDE

In this late hour, God wants to know if we will heed his warnings once our eyes are opened. Spiritual hirelings and dictators do not represent God in any way. God is going to put an end to it all, and when he judges these false leaders, he will continue with the rest of his house. We must hear his clarion call.

When Jesus said that many will be deceived in the last days, he meant they would be spiritually blinded and unable to recognize the difference between truth and a lie. In the gospel of Matthew, Jesus said that "every plant that my heavenly Father has not planted will be pulled up by the roots. Leave them; they are blind guides" (Matt. 15:13–14). Any ministry that does not exalt the name of Jesus Christ and has not been commissioned by the Father will ultimately be destroyed.

Many pastors will soon stand in judgment because not only did they refuse to sound the alarm when they saw the wolves eyeing the crowds, but they joined them in destroying the flock. They invited deceivers into their pulpits while knowing they were teaching false doctrine. According to Jeremiah chapter 23, which many biblical students believe is the cornerstone chapter of Jeremiah's declarations, God points the issues with false prophets directly at the shepherds. God indicts the shepherds for their carelessness in inviting these predators into pulpits to destroy the lives of the sheep. It is the pastors who have given these wolves access to God's people. The increase of false prophets is an indicator that pastors have compromised and joined themselves to partner with the work of Satan. As a result of such alliances, the doors are being opened to spirits that entice the people as they did in Jeremiah's time.

The second letter of Peter addresses the issue of false teachers and evildoers who lure the flock away from Christ by catering to the lust for money (2 Pet. 2:12–22). Sadly, the results of such a lethal merger is that people who had escaped sin are worse off later than in the beginning. Such problems are far more rampant today than when Peter wrote. It is vital that we are enabled to discern truth from error because as time draws to a close, things will only deteriorate with more wolves circling the flock, motivated by evil spirits who are out to kill, steal and destroy. "Evil men and imposters will go from bad to worse, deceiving and being deceived" (2 Tim. 3:13).

God has become weary. He is about to raise up a holy zeal against false teachers, just as he did in Jesus' day. Standing on the temple stairs, the Lord shouted at the leaders, "How dare you turn my Father's house into a market!" (John 2:16). What we see too much of in our churches today is leadership more interested in attaining wealth than in ministering to the body of Christ. Rather than caring about the destination of the people's souls, corrupt and evil men devour every cent they can get by preaching a twisted and self-centered message.

## A TIMELY QUESTION

Why is it we often fail to leave illegitimate teachers? The answer is more complex than we might think.

People stay in churches with dangerous teachers for a variety of reasons, many of which are emotional. If you have ever been involved in a church where, from the outset, people made a place for you, it is easy to fall in love with the people—even if the teaching later proves to be unsound. Especially for desperately lonely people, relationships are so important that they may decide to overlook other serious problems for the sake of holding onto friendships. But there is no reason good enough to stay if one is sitting under damnable teaching. We can be assured that God will meet our needs elsewhere because he loves us with a tender compassion that knows no bounds.

Some people become involved in churches with powerful pastors because they have unmet emotional needs. Because they have never felt loved by a natural father, they can be easily drawn to a "dynamic" male leader. That is one of the reasons many people follow cult leaders. The leader may have, at one point, in the beginning, helped you out in a moment of great need and you never forgot about the act of generosity. But hirelings and dictators are not inclined to gently father their people by building them up in their most holy faith; in actuality, they make you feel like you owe them. By fostering dependence in their followers, they only reinforce feelings of inadequacy and powerlessness in their victims, to the place where the people feel hopeless and experience despair. And often, even if they do decide to leave, they usually struggle to find somewhere else to go where the pastor is a tangible extension of the gentle heart and hands of God.

Another reason some people choose to stay in churches with untrue teachers is that they hate change. Once we are established in a church, it is painful even to consider searching for a new place of worship. When we are comfortable, and when we know the people, it is difficult to imagine starting over somewhere else, and yet, God is able to meet the need elsewhere. While starting over or adjusting to changes is never easy, God will prepare the way before us and lead us exactly where he wants us to go. The only requirement is that we trust him to do that.

For others, I believe looking at the life of Lot, and what convinced him not to leave when he knew the city of Sodom was wicked, speaks to many in our times. Why Lot failed to leave a bad city are the reasons many fail to leave an unbiblical church. I believe there are several reasons:

- He had made the choice to go live there (Gen. 13:10–13). Lot's carnality caused him to choose a place that externally looked promising but was void of godliness. And even though he was vexed by their everyday conduct (2 Pet. 2:8), he hesitated to leave because he had picked the place. When we chose something, our pride makes it harder to admit we made a bad decision, so we tend to stay in that situation or place, hoping that our fasting and praying can turn such things around. But God is not obligated to respond to such activities if where we are was never his will in the first place.

- He had a position of importance (Gen. 19:1). When the angels entered the city of Sodom they found Lot siting at the gate. In ancient times, those sitting at the gate implied leadership influence in the city. This was the gathering place where men would oversee citizens' issues, negotiate business transactions and handle difficult disputes. For Lot to be accepted in such a high-official position points to his spiritual compromise and worldliness. Many struggle leaving bad churches because they are more loyal to their spiritual titles than they are to obeying Christ. Vacating a title is hard for many, especially since they must start over in a new place where people do not acknowledge your previous position. That is a humbling situation. With a spiritual position comes an image, and when Satan knows that something in you desires some type of acknowledgment through a position, he will make sure the unbiblical leader places you in a position right when you know it is time to leave. This is designed to confuse you, and therefore, your loyalty to the man begins to override your devotion to Christ. Leaving at this point will take a miracle.

- His family was at home there (Gen. 19:12–16). Lot's decision to choose and dwell in such defiled environment not only hindered Lot but also his family. Exposing his family to such vile practices caused a division among them. His sons-in-law did not take him seriously, and we know from the rest of the Scriptures that his wife left the city but her heart was really back there, and that unwillingness to let go led to her judgment. Many struggle to depart dishonoring churches because not everyone in the family is in one accord about leaving. The dangerous leader will be skilled at pitting family members against one another, focusing on the one he knows will listen to him. And when there is disagreement, the family usually will stay until everyone reaches a place of peace—but this delay could come with a cost. Ask Lot!

One particular verse of Scripture that's been commonly misinterpreted is in the book of John chapter 10. Jesus said, "The thief does not come except to steal, and to kill, and to destroy. I have come that they may have life, and that they may have it more abundantly" (v. 10). Many have used this verse to highlight the work of Satan, but this verse is not exclusively about Satan. Satan may be the author, but the thief is the method. Jesus was saying that he is the Good Shepherd that gives life, and the thieves, illegitimate leadership, are deceptive shepherds who take life from the sheep. These thieves use trickery to take you captive and rob you of abundance—from the Greek word *zoe,* which means spiritual life—that is in Christ Jesus. Paul tells the believers in Colossians 2:8, "Beware lest anyone cheat you through philosophy and empty deceit, according to the tradition of men, according to the basic principles of the world, and not according to Christ."

When we refuse to leave toxic churches, the truth that is valuable to our spiritual walk is in serious jeopardy. Our adversary is ruthless; and destroying lives in the name of Christ is his objective. But at some point we have to take a good look at ourselves and ask, "Am I helping to strengthen the hands of the Enemy?" We can by allowing loyalty to keep us in something that is not only harmful to our salvation but to our families. Remember loyalty is a great trait, but it can also be lethal. True loyalty is built on truth, but blind loyalty will support a lie.

Pray and ask God for courage and obedience. Ask yourself if it is time to leave a church where destructive and unbiblical teachings are being proclaimed. Again, be aware that when God speaks, some loved ones may not follow. Unfortunately, no one can make their choice for them. Like Lot's wife (Gen. 19:26), they have to decide for themselves.

Though we cannot force others to do what is right, we can warn them and pray for them while there is still time. But no matter what others decide, it is time for us to take heed of the warning to flee. Judgment is at the door.

. . .

## WHAT'S NEXT AFTER THE HURT

As a pastor of a local church, I constantly remind those who are under my care that truth will demand diligent repetition because at any moment we are all capable of believing a repackaged lie and allowing the hurt we experience to override God's principles.

For this reason, it's important for us to make sure that we don't misuse or over sensationalize the true meaning of the words, "spiritual abuse." Often times, many people tend to use the right terminology but have the wrong definition; therefore, they apply the meaning to anything they personally don't agree with.

As mentioned previously, spiritual abuse is the misuse of one's position of power, influence and oversight to promote the self-centered desires or interests of someone other than the individual who is relying on the help. It is when one is not functioning as a leader who serves, but instead uses authority to lord it over others and to foster and defend his own personal vision or needs. When we have experienced hurt or even read or heard stories from others, if we are not careful, it could develop within us a bad eye that views everything from a point of unjust criticism.

For example, just because a leader doesn't do things that I desire for them to do, or even in the manner of what I believe, doesn't mean it's considered abuse. The truth is we will not always agree with everything that takes place within the church; still, not all circumstances are under the umbrella of spiritual abuse.

But when God finally exposes spiritual abuse, we must know that his desire is not for us to continue on, trying to figure out life on our own. In fact, God will not bring judgment to unhealthy leadership unless he has a replacement in mind. Even though unhealthy leadership is a poor reflection of Christ, it does not mean God is through with the church and leadership as a whole.

The challenge after experiencing spiritual abuse will be when you find a sound, biblical church with healthy leadership, and a circumstance arises. The trial will appear when a direction is taken that you personally don't think is acceptable. What will be your response? Keep in mind, Satan never sits idly while we seek to recover from hurt. His plan is to actually make sure the bitter taste church hurt has left in our mouths forever lingers.

This is why evaluation, followed by safeguarding, must happen from the time God removes you from under bad leadership to the moment he directs you to a biblical church. During this moment, we must:

- Seek mature counsel. Sometimes, counsel from outside your circle is what you need to get a clearer view of what's happening in your life. Advice from friends can be distorted if their counsel is laced with bias; think of Rehoboam in 1 Kings 12:1–8. Schedule an appointment with a godly leader to express your fears and concerns—someone who has faithfully navigated through the tough terrain of hurt.
- Refuse to live in your imagination. Satan loves to fish in a mind that's disturbed, distracted and doubtful. He loves to torment those who are overcome with shame for believing something was of God and it was not. Many cannot recover after discovering they were blind to the reality before them. And this is what Satan desires: He wants to hinder our recovery and make it hard for us to ever trust again—*but don't take the bait.* Continue to put your trust in God, knowing that if he pulled you out,

he has the power to see you through so that you can truly experience him.

- Don't attempt to do this on your own. As humans, when we are hurt, our coping mechanism is isolation. But we must be careful that an unbiblical diagnosis is not produced. Hurt has the potential to create an avenue for your mind to generate views that are not true. Stay connected to the Word of God and remain humble so that you may be able to receive instruction in the midst of how you feel. Let us not become like Elijah who was disappointed, and therefore, isolated himself and left his servant behind (1 Kings 19:1–16). When God confronted him, Elijah could not hear God's counsel while in his condition. If disappointment and hurt can offend someone as strong as Elijah, what does that say about someone who doesn't possess as much strength?

- Reevaluate your theology. We usually classify spiritual abuse by what we experience. But truthfully speaking, anytime we are drawn to anything considered ministry, and it's not built on the Word of God, we are subjecting ourselves to abuse. All spiritual abuse begins when God's Word has been neglected, distorted and mishandled. From the moment Scripture is taken out of context, abuse has begun. Reevaluating your theology gives you a proper understanding of who God is, how to properly interpret his Word and insight on how he desires for his church to function.

## The Importance of True Healing

Spiritual healing is more vital than we think. This truth is best supported by Proverbs 4:23–27:

"Guard your heart above all else, for it determines the course of your life. Avoid all perverse talk; stay away from corrupt speech. Look straight ahead, and fix your eyes on what lies before you. Mark out a straight path for your feet; stay on the safe path. Don't get sidetracked; keep your feet from following evil" (NLT).

Even in the midst of God delivering us from something that is painful, we now have a responsibility to pursue our healing. This is made possible through seeking freedom from the offense, malice, bitterness and anger that may have settled in our hearts as a result of what we have experienced. A pure heart is paramount; therefore, we must make every effort to protect ourselves from danger that will come through different avenues. A lack of responsibility on our part can cause an offended heart to lead us—and others—down a destructive path that God never intended for our lives.

On this Christian journey, there will be many pitfalls and obstacles that we must overcome and endure through. Church hurt and betrayal is, unfortunately, part of the list. But what we consider church hurt, God can allow as a method to deliver us out of something we shouldn't have been in. In fact, the good news is that in God's sovereignty, even what we consider to be painful, he has a way of working it out so it can be purposeful. This is why we must make every effort to maintain a pure heart so that we don't find ourselves reliving our past. Christ's desire is for us to look ahead at the joy set before us and not be distracted by the pain that is now behind us.

# A NOTE FROM TAVARES ROBINSON

I am thrilled to offer my readers the tools to help them discern the difference between true shepherds, hirelings and dictators. I pray that God will open many eyes to the truth and bring his people out of false teaching into his marvelous light, where there is restoration, healing and encouragement to walk in the light as he is in the light. May God richly bless you and yours and use you to lift up the marvelous name of Jesus!

# ABOUT THE AUTHOR

Tavares D. Robinson is the founder and senior pastor of Sound the Trumpet Ministries of Miami, located in Miami, Florida, where he has served for fifteen years. He also currently serves as the founder of Watchman Publishing. The Lord has graced Robinson with a bold prophetic voice that turns the hearts of people back to God. He is the author of four previous books: *Shepherds, Hirelings and Dictators: How to Recognize the Difference (first edition)*, *The Utopia of a Strange Love: When the Love of God is Mishandled*, *Warnings from the Garden: Uncovering the Wiles of Deception*, and *The Process of Transition: Reforming the Heart for Growth*. While each of Robinson's books has its own specific focus, they all provide believers with necessary tools to identify truth and discern authentic leadership from spiritually unhealthy leadership. Robinson currently lives with his family in South Florida.

**The Process of Transition: Reforming the Heart for Growth**

ISBN 978-1732513440

Pastor Robinson details the process of the believer's life as a necessary step for growth. He recalls a statement from a neighbor who is a pilot: "For us as pilots, it's all about the journey, but for passengers, it's all about the destination." Believers are often impatient and desire results immediately. But Robinson explains the four steps to becoming transformed by God's work in our lives: detachment, disidentification, disappointment and disconcertment. What do these four steps lead to? Transformation. But when? This book highlights God's promise to those who persevere.

*"A tell all that shines light on the real path to truly becoming transformed in God"*

# The Utopia of a Strange Love: When the Love of God Is Mishandled

ISBN 978-1732513402

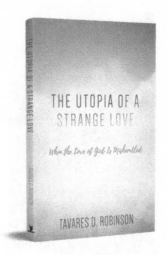

They are ubiquitous these days—eloquent, charismatic preachers, speakers, teachers, and evangelists who skillfully argue that the essential message of Christianity is love. But there are other fundamentals of being a follower of Christ that the popular preachers often ignore. The lack of teaching on it is not just misleading but dangerous. In this book, Pastor Robinson identifies, explores, and discusses the problem, and challenges readers to get back to the basics in order to recover the true historical meaning of God's love.

*"...will take you back to a biblical love of God that is discerning, dividing truth from the lie, where the love of God pushes you out of the realms of comfortable man-made concepts..."*

# Warnings from the Garden: Uncovering the Wiles of Deception

ISBN 978-1732513426

The problem of deception and bowing to the culture goes all the way back to the Garden of Eden, where Adam and Eve became the Serpent's first victims. They began to see circumstances, themselves, and life in general from Satan's point of view, and God's authority was no longer the centerpiece of their lives. This book addresses the many landmines our Adversary has planted among us. It will also help readers uncover errors and recover a passion for historical biblical truths, producing a true conformity to Christ.

*"A must read if you yearn for a bold voice on this topic in the midst of theologically censored, commercialized, seeker-friendly fluff."*

CPSIA information can be obtained
at www.ICGtesting.com
Printed in the USA
LVHW021517300520
656909LV00006B/844

9 781732 513464